The Comic Self

Thinking Theory
Grant Farred, Series Editor

The Comic Self:
Toward Dispossession
Timothy Campbell and Grant Farred

Glissant and the Middle Passage:
Philosophy, Beginning, Abyss
John E. Drabinski

An Essay for Ezra:
Racial Terror in America
Grant Farred

Curating as Ethics
Jean-Paul Martinon

Fates of the Performative:
From the Linguistic Turn to the New Materialism
Jeffrey T. Nealon

The Comic Self

Toward Dispossession

Timothy Campbell and Grant Farred

THINKING THEORY

University of Minnesota Press
Minneapolis
London

MINNESOTA

The University of Minnesota Press gratefully acknowledges financial support for the publication of this series from Cornell University.

Portions of the Introduction were originally published as "Leaving Tragedy: The Comic Self and Possession," *Studi di estetica* 48, no. 4 (March 2020): 31–46, https://doi.org/10.7413/18258646135.

Published by the University of Minnesota Press
111 Third Avenue South, Suite 290
Minneapolis, MN 55401–2520
http://www.upress.umn.edu

ISBN 978-1-5179-1491-2 (hc)
ISBN 978-1-5179-1492-9 (pb)

A Cataloging-in-Publication record for this book is available from the Library of Congress.

Printed in the United States of America on acid-free paper

The University of Minnesota is an equal-opportunity educator and employer.

UMP BMB 2023

For *Alex*
writer, comedy aficionado, razor-sharp wit

and for
Michela, Ale, and Nico

Contents

Preface The Art of Self-Dispossession   ix

Introduction The Fallacy of Self-Possession   1

1. The Sunset of the Self   10
2. Renunciation and Refusal = Rupture and Rapture   18
3. Elide Tragedy   26
4. The Comic Self Is Not Comic   32
5. "I Think"   47
6. David Hume: The Master Critic of Identity   52
7. Temporality contra *Cogito Ergo Sum*   67
8. From a Terminal Walk to a Tightrope Walker   75
9. Don Quijote's Comic Selves   82
10. The Unequal   92
11. Tragic Repetition   100

Acknowledgments   111

Notes   113

Index

Preface
The Art of Self-Dispossession

We owe *The Comic Self* to Michel Foucault, specifically to that moment when he takes leave of the subject in favor of the self. It occurs when he shifts his attention away from the subject to the "forms of subjectivation" by which the individual is "called upon"—the words are Foucault's—"to constitute him or herself as a moral subject."[1] What, we wondered, if the constitution of which Foucault speaks could be extended from the realm of truth and morality to the realm of ownership? Foucault, after all, suggests as much in those pages from *The Birth of Biopolitics* in which he sketches how neoliberalism calls us to mine our own psychic, physical, and biological capital by positing a self that eases the harvesting of individual capital.[2] What, our thinking continued, if the relationality that Foucault saw at the heart of the creation of moral subjects was equally, and perhaps most especially, the seminal move by which individuals were made into productive subjects of capital? Could we locate the precise move by which capital, biopower, neoliberalism, call it what you will, grabs hold of the individual in that moment when the self is possessed by the individual as properly his or her own? Could we employ Foucault's pragmatics of the self as a radical critique of capitalism to the degree that it weakens the ownership of individual over self?

To be clear, much as we pursued these lines of inquiry, these questions, certainly not by themselves, failed to lead directly to the concept of the comic self. And here we took our leave of Foucault simply because we found that he was not much help even as his insight into the power of self-creation provided us with an incentive to explore the relation of possession and self. The point at which we parted ways with Foucault is that precise moment when he mounts his defense of possessing the self, a defense required by wisdom practices in order for care to occur. A further issue, if we are honest, was Foucault's utter lack of interest in possession as a feature of discipline, biopolitics, or even madness.

The problem, to be blunt, is that Foucault is not incisive enough on the crucial question that animates *The Comic Self*: how to think and critique the relation of private property to ownership of the self and others. To our way of thinking, the central weakness of the Foucauldian notion of "care for the self" lies in the missed opportunity to challenge care on the grounds of property—that is, the proprietariness that founds the notion of self-possession. Indeed, care may be exactly what is not needed, and definitely not at this moment in which we find ourselves. It is not needed because it reinforces the tyranny of ownership.

The question of ownership has become meaningful to us in our individual pursuits: Tim's work on forms of generous giving in cinema and Grant's on Heidegger and jazz. However, what marks our individual and, here, collective, pursuits is the desire to understand private property as constituting the very root of all our social ills. Coauthoring *The Comic Self* has had the effect of making clear how the veins of this social ill run deeper and extend further than we were able to see before our collaboration. Some of the change in our collective perspective on possession is surely related to the reconfiguration—the word is not ours—of the humanities that seems everywhere afoot, and only with deleterious effects for the work of thinking. Our concern with the proprietary self also has to do with the way identity—variously laid claim to as "I," "me," "mine," "self"—has come to be treated as a form of property. A form of property, moreover, that must be owned in order to be defended—as in, "This is mine."

It follows, then, that if the root of the problem is private property, then the first relation of ownership will be found in the way subjects relate to their individual self through ownership—as in, most obviously when we say, "This belongs to me." It is out of this, dare one say, fecund soil of pervasive proprietariness that our interest in the self emerges. This, however, does not account for our interest in, and what could perhaps be described as our compulsion with, the comic.

Allow us to explain.

On the one hand, that we would take up the comic is not at all surprising. Interest in the comic—*nota bene* the comic and not comedy— has been steady over the last decade, with works appearing regularly on its generic features across different periods. Some of the most interesting work has appeared in relation to ancient wisdom practices, while the steady flow of scholarship on *commedia dell'arte* continues, as do treatments of the comic in cinema, and of course stand-up comedy, to say nothing of the many eclectic frames that are available to us as well: the psychoanalytic one that Žižek features in his work, including his recent, eclectic take on the pandemic; Alenka Zupančič, in her counterintuitively named *The Odd One In,* offers another; the comic, philosophically rendered, features prominently in the writings of Simon Critchley; and then there is the terrific 2017 *Critical Inquiry* volume.[3]

On the other hand—and this is the point that bears repeating—none of these writers or volumes link the comic to the self through property and ownership. We get glimpses of it from time to time, but our sense is that tragedy is the go-to drug when speaking of ownership. The hegemony of tragedy could function as a kind of shorthand for our critique.

When we speak of tragedy (our tragic loss of the commons, the tragic effects of neoliberalism, for which Foucault may or may not bear some responsibility), we often ignore its dialectical response—that is, we neglect comic dispossession. *The Comic Self* is an attempt to position ourselves on the lost side of the dialectic, as it were.

We do so recognizing that locating a genealogy of the comic self is treacherous. As soon as one begins to trace—the word gives away who and what lies at the origins of the comic self—such a genealogy, one risks fixing the comic self as a conceptual persona (and in this regard Deleuze and Guattari's *What Is Philosophy?* is not useful, though another text is) whose features can be found, named, and then passed over. With that said, we can point to at least two genealogical lines, both of which resolve in contemporary Nietzschean perspectives. The first lies in Jacques Derrida's reading of style in those pages of *Spurs* in which he not only deconstructs the notion of the proper but reconstructs it in a reading of woman: "Either, at times, woman is woman because she gives, because she gives herself, while the man for his part takes, possesses, indeed takes possession."[4] The comic self in such an iteration will be the woman who dispossesses the taking of possession while giving (her-)self away.

The second vein runs from a Nietzschean source as well, and it is one that we feature nearly from the first page of this book. Gilles Deleuze in *Difference and Repetition* distinguishes between comic and tragic repetitions:

> The difference between the comic and the tragic pertains to two elements: first, the nature of the repressed knowledge—in the one case immediate natural knowledge, a simple given of common sense, in the other terrible esoteric knowledge; second, as a result, the manner in which the character is excluded from this knowledge, the manner in which "he does not know that he knows."[5]

The ways in which Deleuze links repetition to the comic allow us to flesh out some of the most important features for our comic self: the comic self repeats comically, by which we mean repeats the gesture of dispossession, understanding that all attempts at dispossession fail. Out of this self-same gesture emerges the recognition that all attempts at self-possession too must end in failure.

They fail precisely because there is no comic repetition without its tragic antithesis (and vice versa), without incessant attempts to possess the self as my own. Attempts at pinpointing the precise traits of the comic self will be challenging, and that is because when we arrive at what we take to be the scene of the origin of the comic self, we find ourselves chasing a shadow. We arrive at the scene of origin at the precise moment that the comic self withdraws. It can only be seen in glimpses, in those fleeting moments just before it reverts to the tragic possession of an I. An I that, following Deleuze, thinks it knows what the self truly is.

The task that the comic self assigns us is therefore onerous. It insists above all on the importance of sharpening our attention and reflexes so that we can see where, how, and when the comic self is manifested. It was a surprise, therefore, to discover that the more we turned to philosophy, the more stymied were our attempts to track it down. It was then that we shifted to literature. In so doing, we surprised ourselves by turning at a work that we could not have imagined featuring—so centrally—at the outset: Miguel de Cervantes's *Don Quijote*. There are many reasons that may explicate why literature seems able to hold open longer the window on the comic self. Perhaps, as Roland Barthes writes, it has to do with literature's inclination to baffle the place of mastery.[6] Our readings of *Don Quijote* and Virginia Woolf, among others, reflect our attention on how literature confounds our attempts at naming once and for all who or what the comic self is. Another way of putting this would be to recognize that dispossessing ourselves à la the comic self must—whether or not we like it, or no matter how much we may dislike it—involve embracing literature's baffling qualities. Strangely, or maybe not so strangely, literature liberates us into dispossession. Or, as can be said of our invocations of Franz Kafka's work, literature liberates us into limited possession. We understand that Kafka has a great deal to say about dispossession and, what is more, is possessed of a keen insight into the distinction between I and mine. However, since Kafka's series of insights always tend toward the tragic, our turn to Kafka is strategic rather than extended. Unfairly, no doubt, Kafka serves mainly as a dialectical foil for, in the main, Miguel Cervantes and Shakespeare, although Kafka features more prominently, obviously, in our discussion on metamorphosis. Even then his Gregor Samsa is coupled, again, unfairly, with a markedly lesser literary personage, Polonius ("Alas, poor Gregor"). It is simply wrong that Gregor finds himself saddled with so flimsy—if provocative, and then only as a consequence of his failures—a literary counterpart. A second "alas" that does not make things, no doubt because of its repetition, any better.

Duly liberated, we are free to turn our focus away from tragedy. As we have argued, when we focus on tragedy, we miss what the comic self brings to light, and that is the self. Both neoliberal subjectivity and its critiques gloss over this crucial point, hence our shift to critiquing the decisive role played by possession and property, and the need to practice dispossession of that first piece of property that we have, own, and believe ourselves to be: the self.

In this regard we draw, more implicitly rather than explicitly, and rarely in a sustained way, on the impolitical—especially as we acknowledge the need for an impolitical reading of the self and politics and how both continue to deflect from practices of dispossession. A number of

Italian philosophers, most notably Roberto Esposito, elaborated the category of the impolitical thirty years ago, and it is perhaps most famously featured in Giorgio Agamben's most overtly political work from the 1990s, *The Coming Community*. An intriguing term, the impolitical names the process or movement whereby representations of order and political life ironically have the effect of lessening conflict among subjects, populations, and individuals. *The Comic Self* contributes to an impolitical critique by showing how the principal conflict that the political fails to order is the relation of subject to self. To speak of the comic self is to locate the central conflict for today within struggles around possession, which originate, in our view, in the relation of individual to self.

Finally, a word on how we collaborated in writing *The Comic Self.* At an early stage, it became clear that the kind of voice we wanted and needed for a book on the perils of ownership, as well as the inevitability of possession, would be markedly different from our individual efforts. It would have to be a joining and a sundering of our voices in a style in which neither of us "takes possession" of what the other has written or thought. What we discovered, the more we wrote, was a style that neither of us recognized completely; more direct, alienating, and violent than what we surely would have produced on our own. So be it.

The Comic Self lacerates and is lacerating, hardly what we expected at the outset but what we are glad of having achieved. Indeed, that may be our central and unsettling insight. We are so entangled in ownership that the move to disentangle brings unexpected joys as well as other less sightly things.

The Comic Self is, as such, the best book we never wrote.

Introduction
The Fallacy of Self-Possession

There is nothing natural or necessary in the identification of self and own, thanks to which being oneself can no longer be separated from owning oneself. The identification is merely a postulate, not an injunction.
—ÉTIENNE BALIBAR, "'My Self,' 'My Own': Variations on Locke"

"The comic self? Really?" a skeptical reader might wonder upon opening this book. Is there really the need for another conceptual persona meant to uncover again something previously ignored in contemporary reality, society, subjectivity? Another reader, less suspicious perhaps, musters patience, ready to challenge the idea of bringing the comic and self together, recalling other attempts, other itineraries whose destination is clear enough. If this is going to be another translation of the practices of the self that Michel Foucault spoke about forty years ago, then say so. A third reader peeks out from behind the other two, more sympathetic potentially to the cause of the comic self, perhaps because she hears in it an acknowledgment to beloved pages from another philosopher who, in the dialectic between comic and tragic repetition, updated a reading of Marx's *Eighteenth Brumaire* about history repeating itself. Is that what this is going to be? If it is, then admit it, since as Deleuze himself knew there is nothing as tiresome as acting as if something were not self-evident, especially when the topic is knowing the self.[1]

Which reader has it right? We are not going to answer, at least not yet. But we will say that yes, what follows is a reading of an increasingly visible conceptual persona called the comic self that, in our view, responds philosophically to the contemporary moment in ways that merit attention. And yes, a relation to a Foucauldian practice of the self bubbles below the surface here, though it is decidedly not in the realm of care. And yes, comic and tragic repetition lie at the fractured origin of our reading of a form of the self we call the comic. It is all of these and none since at its heart we are attempting to introduce a figure whose visibility allows us to ask questions about the political and subjective drama of today—a visibility that is rarely continuous given that we cannot make it our own, as its function is precisely to unsettle our notions of being and having.

That we find ourselves signing off on comedy and the self speaks to the current upside-down moment when violence is not just in the air but on the ground, when a pandemic has made clear just how many of our previous modes of thinking the relation of the individual to the self are not just simply antiquated but harmful for democratic and political life. The recent history of the fortunes of comedy and the comic is instructive. Clearly, there has been a discernible inflation around the terms ever since a killer clown was elected president in 2016, though it is also true that interest in the comic appeared earlier.[2] When people think of the comic today, they likely have in mind stand-up comics and comedians on Tik-Tok or Netflix, gifted in the art of parody, satire, and necessary ridicule. As for the self, the story is longer, dicier, and notoriously more unsettled. The self has been playing nasty tricks on philosophers nearly from the moment that philosophy itself was born. Leaving aside definitions new, quaint, and ancient for now, the self began its reemergence some fifty years ago in a restoration that continues today, thanks to the work of Michel Foucault, who, in the final volumes of *The History of Sexuality* and a series of lectures at the Collège de France, reintroduced the self and its care as a mode for thinking subjectivization. We will have much more to say about care and the self and the problems that emerge when associating the two, but what matters is how, by bringing the comic and self together, a different conceptual space for thinking becomes available.

Often appearing surreptitiously in thought, the comic self names a form of relationality, though by no means the only one, in which an individual engages with the self so that dispossession becomes available as a subjective tactic to weaken the relation of ownership between individual and self. Unnamed and unnoticed, the comic self lurks in a specific set of philosophical discourses, blunting them at moments when the fallacy of self-possession is most present. The task we have given ourselves in the pages that follow is to show how the comic self undoes them by indicating how much of the authority of these concepts rests on self-possession as "natural or necessary." Again, if there is a critique linked to the comic self, it will proceed in the direction of dispossession.

What does it mean to dispossess? In our definition, to dispossess means to disentangle the I from mine or I from my own. The means for doing so remain relatively stable across centuries and thinkers, its chief mode involving the adopting of a particular attitude to knowing. A rhetoric and a typology follow, which we link in the opening chapters to the figures of anadiplosis and chiasmus, each founded on an affinity for repetition and recollection. As we hope to show, when the comic self laughs, what it laughs at most, often loudly, is the fallacy of self-possession, as it remembers how often it fails to follow its own advice.[3]

To take up the comic self as the figure for thinking dispossession, some preliminary work is in order, especially as it concerns the key protagonists that the comic self faces off against and the various equipment, philosophical and attitudinal, that the comic self will need. Some highlights follow below.

The Comic Self, the Tragic Self

The comic self does not exist in isolation as it emerges in contradistinction to another figure, the tragic self. Not just a foil, the tragic self names the individual who has confused ownership with identity, who relates to the self as if the self were some thing, some commodity that belongs to it. There are other less self-evident names we might employ to describe the contemporary tragic self—indeed, so much of how we speak of the self, even when we care for it, is couched in terms of tragedy, names such as entrepreneur, neoliberal subjects, influencers come to mind—but what they all have in common is a confusion around identity and ownership. The comic self does not hesitate to laugh at these individual owners. Indeed,

much of its laughter derives from the self's inability to disavow possession.

However, true to its dialectical nature, the comic self is not simply
at opposite ends from its tragic doppelgänger, but it does from time to
time recognize their similarities, especially in moments when the comic
self comes up short in its attempts to dispossess. The constitutive difference between the two resides in their attitude toward possession. This is
entirely of a piece with our argument that the comic self speaks to and
against its tragic counterpart, when the difficulty that is dispossession
presents itself as most urgent.

If we were to translate the comic self into aesthetic terms that Hege-
lians among us might recognize, we might say that the comic self allows
us to see not the complete dissolution of capitalism as a religion à la Walter Benjamin but the pervasive hold that possession as ownership has on
us today—the way that we continue to confuse I with mine. This confusion represents the highlight or the triumph of a certain kind of subjectivity based on tragedy. If only the I could separate itself from mine, it
could adopt an ethical life as its essence. But it cannot because tragedy is
one-dimensional in the way it treats the individuality of the self. There
is no depth, as Hegel reminds us repeatedly, no individuality where tragedy is concerned. The comic self offers a different mode of relating to
the necessity of ethical life by embracing "subjective caprice," a "mode of
plasticity," that takes up the absurd position that the self can be dispossessed.[4] Hence, in our reading the comic self stands in for a subjective
caprice—with all of the hints of a Deleuzian becoming-animal that this
entails—that gives in to the impulse to provocation in order to see more
urgently than we have up to now how destructive the confusion of I and
mine has become.[5] Yes, Hegel's work on comedy and tragedy in the *Aesthetics* subtends much of our thinking on the comic self, but our Hegel,
however, has a decidedly Deleuzian cast. Ours is figured so mainly because of the way in which Deleuze enables us to dissolve Hegel's tragedy/
comedy distinction, thereby allowing us to present the comic self in its
full complexity, our eye firmly set on the dissolution rather than the resolution of Hegel's dyad.

Why so much interest in possession? Our answer is clear. Show us
another relationship that looms so large over politics, the environment,

life itself. Is there anything, any life, any identity that cannot be owned? Where are they? Who does the owning? The comic self speaks for the tragic self by overwhelming it with the facticity and command of dispossession because it knows the answer to these questions.

Dispossession

The comic self is constitutively antithetical to any attempt to represent itself as incorporated or neatly insulated. It is, to borrow a term dear to contemporary Italian thought, impolitical as it evades representation at every turn.[6] Given this genealogy, it is not surprising that the comic self resonates with one of the definitions Jacques Derrida attributes the term spur: "The style-spur, the spurring style, is a long object, an oblong object, a word, which perforates even as it parries."[7] In its relation to the tragic self, the comic "perforates" as much as it is "perforated"; it seeks to guard against "intrusion" by the tragic self, as much as the latter works to maintain its integrity, and so both undertake to "parry" or "spurn" the other. Vulnerability and openness to the other are mutual and yet both are indefatigably part of how each self encounters the other.

Such an openness extends widely. The comic self is a singularity uncomposed of synchronized elements, each complementing the other, somehow operating in harmony. Not an automaton, the comic self rather makes difference immanent across a range of registers. One of those immanences, to return to Derrida and the spur, will return as "the woman's figure" in a discussion of "sexual difference."[8] At its core, the comic self names an unrepresentable composition of forces, is constituted by the conflict among them, and out of this conflict is able to generate its enormous power of perforation.

The Grammar of Dispossession

To possess is unremarkable. As a grammatical structure, self-possession is the stuff of day-to-day life. We might pronounce it as, say, "I would like to get that back, please. It is mine."[9] This is a structure of possession that we could reformulate infinitely. We declare, "That is mine." Furthermore, we freely recalibrate the language of possession as much as we are inclined to, tailoring it to the idiom of our choice: "I want what is mine." We submit it to reconstruction after reconstruction. In an argument, when aspersion is cast upon us (we are presumed uncertain, hesitant, unsure of ourselves), it might emerge, defensively, as "I know my own mind." It could as easily function as an assertion of self in a graduate seminar or in a family disagreement. "I know my own mind" is a phrase, like the others, that has many uses. It is adaptable to its context, flexible and creative in its deployment.

Toddlers, in feeling their way to language and taking their first philosophically fatal stabs toward self-possession, are sometimes known to say, when an adult intervenes or proposes another course of action, "I am the boss of me." Is this a primal form of self-possession ever unlearned? Or does it simply assume more subtle and articulate forms? Is self-possession the champion of linguistic disguise? The überdissembler? The refusal to be "separated from owning oneself" begins early, after which it continues unabated, naturalized by the frequency of everyday usage, where naturalization is deemed indivisible from necessity. From, say, the cultural necessity that is *Me Myself I,* the title track of Joan Armatrading's 1980 album.[10] Armatrading's is a single, continuous, and unambiguous claim to self-possession, the multiple folding into one/One and in so doing rigorously reinforcing the self's possession of itself. That you can dance to the track with no Rosa Luxemburg guilt attached is not to be undervalued. How much more clearly can the facticity of self-possession be enunciated? If we include the Armatrading title, we can parenthesize what we noted above. Étienne Balibar does not dwell on the run-of-the-mill articulation, but neither can he leave it unremarked, a sure sign of its importance. For Balibar, self-possession is a "conflict that cannot be resolved in everyday life, only masked or avoided."[11] "Self-possession" is indeed the very stuff of "everyday life." In "everyday life," as much as or maybe more than anywhere else, the self is presumed to, unquestionably, "own" itself, as if it had no other choice. As if self-possession simply is. As if, à la Armatrading, it is a run-on phrase: "Me Myself I," no punctuation necessary.

What is recognized as the fallacy of self-possession in the toddler, a fallacy identifiable in language, is accepted as de rigueur in the language of everyone else. How unreflectively "I am the boss of me" mutates into "I am what is mine." At least the toddler, we can say, is honest about declaring his allegiance to self-possession. He would appear to already know that "being oneself can no longer be separated from owning oneself."[12] Are we all just toddlers, seeking to boss ourselves into the fallacy of self-possession? To be the boss of ourselves, from our earliest possible articulations of self-ownership? What the toddler and the adult (be that Balibar or Armatrading, no matter their different registers) leave us with, then, is the question of how self-possession can, if at all, in young and old, be ruptured.

Rupturousness, Rapturousness

Interior intimo meo. The complete phrase from Augustine is "interior intimo meo et superior summo meo." "Yet all the time you were more inward to me than the most inward place of my heart and loftier than the highest."[13] For a range of scholars, the focus on Augustine's critique of self-knowing is interiority.[14] Étienne Balibar, drawing on Augustine's insight that God has penetrated his "heart," dividing him from within himself, locates this experience as disrupting the "very intimacy of the self."[15] For Augustine, God is the source of the rupture that leads to rapture. In having God take up residence uninvited in the "most inward place of [his] heart," Augustine sets in motion a process that will see him liberated from his Manichean past, from the "shameless woman."[16] In short, because Augustine has confessed his sins, God has orchestrated the rupture from within, setting him on a transcendent, "loftier than the highest," illuminating, God-ordained path, whose every step brings him closer to Him. There remains, as there always is in the case of a spiritual awakening, work to be done; more redolent is the promise of rapture emerging out of rupture.

The comic self too will find its way toward rapture, but to do so it must do the work of repeatedly separating I from mine—a work that is never complete, given the relation of rapturousness to intimacy. For Augustine, rupture marks God's intercession, which produces out of internal division an unbreakable bond between God and self. For the comic self, the toddler's self-possession rearticulates itself in the adolescent and the adult and requires a multilayered vigilance in order to ward off lapsing into the fallacy of self-possession. For the comic self, rapture is not the experience of cohabitation with the divine; it does not amount to a logic that decrees. Instead, the comic self refuses intimacy as possession and so creates conditions for secular rapture, an abduction of the self from the self.

We can state it differently: The comic self knows what it does not know. Achieving this, the comic self's entire relationship to itself is adjusted to knowing-what-it-does-not-know. This in turn produces an attitude in which the comic self knows itself not as the cause of itself. We can offer this as a near tautology: It achieves à la Augustine a state of rapturousness through the rupture enacted by dispossession. Rapturousness emerges out of a rupturousness that acknowledges the persistent merging of both. Need we add that this merging most intensely carries within it the possibility of the ecstatic?

Dispossess!

Where do all of these moments of toddler parenting, parries and perforations, and rupture and rapture lead? To a command: Dispossess! Dispossess what? The answer is clear enough—dispossess the self of the self. We know by now that the problem, humanity's problem, our problem, is possession; it is what alienates us, and so dispossessing ourselves of the self as property becomes the flip side of dispossessing ourselves of the idea (and attitude) that treats the relation as one of ownership. To dispossess is to choose, say, giving (a)way over property, to choose not-knowing over a form of knowing that involves mastery, possession, knowing what I know, and not knowing the incomprehensible vastness that I do not know.

Of course, dispossession never happens all at once: we fail and fail again. Rather than merely saying "dispossess," we need a figure who can square (disposession multiplied by itself) and extend dispossession. The comic self is that figure because it sees, even in its moments of failure, that possession of failure is unavailable. "Dispossess" is the command to dispossess again and again.

The following chapters are attempts to represent the unrepresentable comic self, to muddy the waters around it, around identity, and the practices of the self whose precise weight will not be found in care but in a different relation that may or may not have care of the self at its heart.

To repeat: the problem with care of the self is that it reinforces identity, strengthening the relation between I and this identity that is mine. But this raises a question, one of the most important for today and for how we are to live individually and collectively with each other and ourselves: How can you care for something that is not yours? The comic self ranges across literature, philosophy, and contemporary comedy and in each appearance uncovers a space where dispossession of self and the dismantling of care is possible.

Naturally, our method is more improvisational than interpretive, which means it veers unexpectedly between polemical and poignant. We do not own these readings; the readings are ephemerally dogmatic or dogmatic in their ephemerality. Everyone is so intent on entangling I with mine and me, it makes sense that we would want to use this opportunity for disentangling. What follows, then, is an extended play of spurring the reader and ourselves on to think what we have not thought yet, what we have not lived yet because we continue to prefer our tragic selves to the comic self.

CHAPTER 1

The Sunset of the Self

Although I search myself it's always someone else I see.
—ELTON JOHN, "Don't Let the Sun Go Down on Me"

In the Introduction, we noted how slippery the comic self can be. Just when it seems ready to show itself, it recedes, its unrepresentability matched only by its ability to puncture all attempts at recognition. Why? What is it that lends it such power? Lacan recounts memorably a stage in which the self of the child comes to recognize himself in the mirror-stage: "The child, at an age when he is for a time, however short, outdone by the chimpanzee in instrumental intelligence, can already recognize as such his own image in a mirror."[1] The child, who can be as young as six months, is entirely capable of apprehending an image of himself. The comic self is not this child. As Elton John diagnoses it, what is being made visible in the mirror-stage is of a distinct order: "It's always someone else I see." Where the child is certain about what and who is being seen, the comic self knows the score. It recognizes a rupture between the "I" that "searches" for itself and the "someone else" it, as a matter of course, encounters. It knows that the self is always to be "searched for" and it is this that explains its power to frustrate any attempts by the individual to gain access to it.

What does the I of the comic self see if it only sees someone else? On the one hand, it sees what is not-I; on the other, it knows that the someone else it sees is not it. To see others and to know that they are not me already suggests that there is a way to think possession outside of subject, since the "I" can only be approached as not "someone else." This happens at the moment when "someone else" is made visible and is based on the understanding that every encounter with this misnamed figure, "someone else," begins with an intention that who I truly am can be retrieved from what I am not. We can say this differently. The I that wants to see presumes that the self it longs to see is someone other than the "someone else" being "seen." Here, perhaps more than at any other moment, the desire to see the self, to encounter it fully, reveals the futility of that desire. Lacan will call this futility of desire "lack"; there is no mode of approach able to arrive at the self. (The self is always denied itself, we would propose, by jouissance of the comic self variety.) When we understand that we cannot make the someone else I see me, possession of self and mine falters. Desire to see the I as belonging to me is unthinkable without anticipating that it is not, already, a priori, me.

This is the dyad, a "double" contracted into I-mine, or I = mine, or I + mine = I, which is repeated again and again, becoming both the ground for the formation of itself and divisible into I and mine. Capable of infinite reconstitution, the reconstitution of the self-same self-identity depends upon the undifferentiated, indistinct I, the I that remains through all experiences, reconstitutable as I. It is precisely this I that lies at the very ground of all our problems with subjectivity.

Anadiplosis

Those writing on the comic self, lacking a name for it, have had to find ways of drawing it and drawing it out. The difficulties are not insignificant since the comic self is continually doubled between this reconstitutable I and mine. One frequent strategy is to adopt the rhetorical figure of anadiplosis, or the duplication of the last word of a period, phrase, or verse at the beginning of the succeeding one.[2] Anadiplosis reinstates, through repetition, I-mine, marking, as such, the return to the self's defensive position: the I is solid and in no need of reconstitution. A defensive position wards off what lurks at the limit where the comic and the self are drawn apart: death.

Kenneth Burke, that most comic of thinkers, describes anadiplosistically how the comic form affects human relations. He acknowledges that an early draft of his magisterial *A Grammar of Motives* was originally conceived as a work of comedy:

> In our original plans for this project, we had no notion of writing a "grammar" at all. We began with a theory of comedy, applied to a treatise on human relations. Feeling that competitive ambition is a drastically over-developed motive in the world, we thought this motive might be transcended if men devoted themselves not so much to "excoriating" it as to "appreciating" it. Accordingly, we began taking notes on the foibles and antics of what we tended to think of as "the Human Barnyard."[3]

We do not in any way wish to suggest that the comic self belongs to the same genre as *A Grammar of Motives*. For our part, we only occasionally attend to the "foibles and antics of . . . 'the Human Barnyard,'" although it must be said that most philosophical treatises would be well served if they added a dollop or two of these. And, like most "theories of comedy," there lurks within it a tragic element, so much so that Burke's "Human Barnyard" puts one in an Orwellian caste of mind. But at the very least, Burke's tone, by turns ironic and lacerating, refracts in the comic self. Indeed, his critique that the "competitive ambition is a drastically over-developed motive in the world" resonates with the comic self's constitutive dispossession. Through his philosophical register, Burke is able to intimate and animate the comic self, revealing the extent to which a "theory of comedy" sometimes lurks at the edge of philosophical discourse.

However, it is for his rendering of the relationship between anadiplosis and form that Burke is of primary interest to us.

> Once you grasp the trend of the form, it invites participation regardless of the subject matter. Formally, you will find yourself swinging along with the succession of antitheses, even though you may not agree with the proposition that is being presented in this form. Or it may even be an opponent's proposition which you resent. Of course, the more violent your original resistance to the proposition, the weaker will be your degree of "surrender" by "collaborating"

with the form. But in cases where a decision is still to be reached, a yielding to the form prepares for assent to the matter identified with it. Thus, you are drawn to the form, not in your capacity as a partisan, but because of some "universal" appeal in it. And this attitude of assent may then be transferred to the matter which happens to be associated with the form.[4]

The comic self reveals repetition across a range of texts, and it does so by employing anadiplosis. Not surprisingly, "architectural" effects ensue, including, most prominently, impending descent.

The architecture of anadiplosis is nowhere more evident than in T. S. Eliot's "The Love Song of J. Alfred Prufrock." Riddled by self-doubt, anadiplosis and chiasmus plague Prufrock at every turn:

> And indeed there will be time
> To wonder, "Do I dare?" and, "Do I dare?"
> Time to turn back and descend the stair,
> With a bald spot in the middle of my hair—
> (They will say: "How his hair is growing thin!")[5]

The metaphor of descent is obvious. Literally coming down the staircase, almost immobilized by the fear of judgment ("'How his hair is growing thin!'"), the time will arrive for a reckoning with descent. What is more, however, is that Eliot alerts us to the inevitability of fatality that appears endemic to anadiplosis. Repetition, as it folds the I back into I having passed through I-mine, resounds as the death knell. In "Prufrock," everything is mediated through the onset of what is understood as the decrepitude of the middle-aged male body. Anadiplosis powers the spiral of and into death. Deleuzian death is what interrupts lines of flight. For its part, anadiplosis marks Prufrock's lines of flight as well as his lines of death:

> We have lingered in the chambers of the sea
> By sea-girls wreathed with seaweed red and brown
> Till human voices wake us, and we drown.[6]

If Eliot sets the scene early to alert us to Prufrock's impending demise, the poet leaves us in no doubt by the end. Here the line of flight manages to procure a soft landing, surrounded by "sea-girls wreathed with seaweed red and brown," the seabed Prufrock's final resting place, we presume. However, it would be difficult to envisage a more absolute descent in "drowning" that seems, for all its gloomy inevitability, to offer something of a respite after having "lingered [for how long?] in the chambers of the sea." A "chamber" on the order of purgatory, true, but this time being consumed by water, somewhat genteelly, rather than living the proximity of fires hellish hot seems the better option: this line of flight, as it were, rather than that line of flight. With his lack of substantiality and his high-level social anxiety (we are free to diagnose him even as an acute neurotic),[7] Prufrock seems more deserving of liquid dissolution rather than fiery consumption.

Anadiplosis is not just a mode of neurosis, mapping a steadily downward trajectory in "Prufrock." In *Julius Caesar,* it manages to achieve, simultaneously, both descent and ascent. Shakespeare does so through the repetition of two terms, honorable man/men (Brutus, but Cassius as well) and ambition (Caesar). The first term is supposedly a recognition of how Brutus's venerability descends into the violence that is commonness; the second is intended as a pejorative and a political indictment by the conspirators and ascends from commonness in a postlapsarian political resurrection, all this because of Mark Antony's skill as political orator. Be careful, Shakespeare suggests, about who is allowed to deliver political eulogies. It takes but a skillful wielding of anadiplosis as a rhetorical weapon to produce political death, on the occasion of acknowledging death and bestowing "honor" on the undeserving dead. It might not be enough, as Burke would have it, "to grasp the trend of the form."[8] How the "subject matter" informs as well as deforms, takes apart, rips asunder, the "form" is what will ultimately decide how the political effects of mobilizing through anadiplosis are manifested. One need only consider how anadiplosis is deployed across social media today to see how easily forms are being retooled for political descent and ascent. In *Julius Caesar,* anadiplosis is what throws I (Caesar and Mark Antony) into a life-and-death struggle with mine (Brutus, Cassius, and the Republicans of Rome who will later be moved to change sides).

We will have more to say about the emergence of the comic self in the play later, but for now it is enough to note that the comic self is not somehow passive where other selves are active. Instead, it is able to enact a break between I and mine (Antony and Brutus) that precipitates violence, setting in motion a descent into dictatorship and an ascent into a state after the failure of the republic in which I no longer reinforces itself by the search for mine among friends, groups, or politicians.

However fallaciously conceived, however swiftly it might be taken apart, however much the inclination to reject it as unsustainable appears, thinking possession is a philosophical event given that the very notion of the self is founded on it. Possession speaks of the indefatigable desire to lay claim to and, indeed, to capture the self—to take hold of, permanently, the self, assuming that such a restraining, restricting, constricting is even possible. More than anything, the self wants to make the self captive in order to possess, without condition or qualification, the undifferentiated I.

This desire to possess the self is founded upon the logic of geomythology, where an imaginary "there," a specific psychopolitical locale, can hold the self in place. In his appreciation of the "restlessness" of the Surrealists, Lacan names this place where "human knowledge is determined" "that 'little reality' [ce peu de réalite]."[9] Such a "little reality" is an inordinately powerful and resonant locale; furthermore, the "little reality" in which the I cannot be contracted into mine "determines" a very different order of the knowledge of self. The comic self does not permit contraction because it eschews any reality that subordinates itself to the logic of contraction. No more powerful narrowing of the I can be found than that around mine.

Incidents in the Life of a Slave Girl

The determination to possess the self turns us toward a kind of captivity narrative, which is unsurprising given the acquire-and-retain thrust that girds possession. This unattainable "there" is where the self can be held in place, as it is for Linda Brent.[10] In Harriet Jacobs's *Incidents in the Life a Slave Girl,* "there" is where the self is confined to a discrete, secret place, against its will, of course. From this place of captivity, writing the self as a form of possession becomes available since writing personally (as opposed to impersonally) will depend upon holding the self captive. To write "I" is to write as if the writing self were the same as "I": it presumes that such a self could be contracted (or expanded, which amounts sometimes to the same thing) into "I." Indeed, Jacobs writes for this reason:

not only to establish possession over the enslaved self but to demonstrate that the enslaved can, in fact, write and, in so doing, write itself. We are confronted with a tautology, which may be more or less useful, depending on the circumstances. There can be no possession that is not self-possession. If self-possession is impossible, then it follows that there could have been, from the very first, no possession of any thing, any object, any other human being, without it. All writing of the self requires an I that is indistinguishable and indivisible from the self.

It is no wonder, then, that this geomythic place is so difficult to locate, so much so that we could easily pronounce it an impossibility since it is the aporia of self-holding. Linda Brent, for instance, can see outside, which means that, from one vantage point or another, it is possible for her to be seen. The attic cannot hold her, her writing attests to this. What lies between her and the world is perforated by physical structure, disposition, and writing. To write is as much about expelling/propelling the self into the world as it is about allowing the world in, beckoning it to come closer. She is open to the world as much as she protrudes into it, through the pen and looking out. If self-possession is unattainable, there is nothing for the self to do but find itself turned back from its search. Once the shock of understanding that "someone else I see" wears off, the self recognizes that there is nowhere to turn but in the direction of what is supposed to be there but is not. The self faces the prospect of turning on its heels, once more, Sisyphus-like, to begin again the impossible work of "searching" for the self.

This turning explains how the self winds up in the company of that famous malaprop, Yogi Berra. Backpedaling from what it cannot possess, the self can do nothing but acknowledge, as that venerable old catcher would have it, that the self's "search" for itself is just "déjà vu all over again." We would be well-advised to give the romantic courage of Sisyphus and the litany of seductive misspeaking that is Yogi Berra a wide berth. We are much better off sticking with Elton John. After all, nostalgia for self-possession is dismissed in that moment when the comic self understands the truth about itself, in that moment when expectations about the self are elided. This truth manifests under very particular conditions: namely, in that moment when the self disappears from view. As it does so, the self assumes a role akin to that of the trickster, transforming all too quickly into unrecognizability before our very eyes, while still holding us, against our better philosophical instincts, in its thrall.

In this moment, the comic self presents itself as a figure familiar to a thinker such as Marx. The self is compelled to function under the sign of elision (ēlisiō), struck out or, as we conceive it here, more elimination than deliberate omission—when it is rendered into private property. Private property is not an act but the state of the exclusion of labor, a fact that we would do well to remind ourselves of daily. In the *Economic and Philosophic Manuscripts of 1844,* Marx renders it this way: "Labour, the subjective essence of private property as exclusion of property, and capital, objective labour as exclusion of labour, constitute private property as it is developed in a state of contradiction."[11] The self as "private property" is a conception that is all too familiar, not only to Marx but to all of us. We can happily join with him, or not, but either way we have no choice but to name it as an ordinary articulation: self-pronunciation. The aspirations of capital coincide with the illusions of the self. The result? "Capital can complete its dominion over man and become, in its most general form, a world-historical power."[12]

Because of Marx and our enduring familiarity with this form of self-proclamation, we can make our claim about elision without fear of contradiction. In asserting the centrality of elision to the comic self, we declare ourselves willing to think the self in terms that are themselves "rapturous" and that refuse any notion of a predestined self.

The comic self announces impatiently: "I disown myself." "I have never owned myself," it continues, "not even as a three-year-old," or, in the mode retroactive of self-refusal: "I disown having ever owned myself." The comic self not only disavows its toddler self but is set against any other conception of self that does not take into account the proposition that is dispossession.

CHAPTER 2

Renunciation and Refusal = Rupture and Rapture

Renunciation

In a 1971 interview, the Italian poet, filmmaker, and philosopher Pier Paolo Pasolini offers a critique of the work of the self that has gone largely unremarked on, one that turns on a tension between the self and the world. In contradistinction to how we traditionally imagine the self, Pasolini presents us instead with a mediocre and heteronormative domestic self. He counterposes these selves in an intensely Jesus-the-Christ vocabulary whose effect is to draw a distinction between "real" and "unreal" selves. In response to a question about how he understands the "renunciation of the self," Pasolini reflects:

> Practically speaking, renunciation of the self, in my opinion, Christ says it immediately after, and that is that one renounces oneself insofar as one carries one's cross each day. The self [il se stesso] of staying at home peacefully, with the wife and kids, trapped in the treadmill of political apathy [qualunquismo] and colorless *bonhomie,* tends not to carry the cross. Whoever carries the cross risks their lives constantly, puts it constantly into jeopardy. To me, that self-renunciation does not mean to renounce oneself as an individual, in the ascetic sense, as mystics would hold, but to renounce a historic, habitual [abitudinario] self is to renounce daily routine, apathy, in short. Christ invites us to dissociate a real self from an unreal self who gets lost in the dream of life

and invites us instead to renounce the latter in order to choose the former, and really be ourselves. I therefore don't have a sense of the Christ of the ascetic moment.[1]

"Renunciation" constitutes a political risk. It is not an aversion to the political "realities" of the everyday or a reverting to "asceticism" but a daily renewal of the commitment to living a political life. It is that life in which even the "dream" of the revolution, of a sanctified life, is the stuff of a repeated and daily labor that is often grinding. The revolution is the dream, mediated through Christology, for which we must work. Taking up the cross, once more, every single day, learning again to make the self worthy of Jesus-the-Christ's sacrifice, is the only safeguard against "political apathy" in Pasolini's view. On the face of it, the comic self has every reason to take its distance from the possessable self of Pasolini's injunction and thus to "really be ourselves."

Equally apparent, however, Pasolini's self who "carries one's cross each day" is itself ruptured and rapturous. The logic of the break with the world, as ascending into rapture contains the very stuff of a certain branch of evangelical Christian eschatology and is the promise made by Paul to the Thessalonians. Writing of how the living and the dead will be reconciled in Jesus-the-Christ, Paul says: "Then we who are alive, who are left, will be caught up in the clouds together with them to meet the Lord in the air."[2] If the rapture promises the ascension that is endemic to those who believe in Jesus-the-Christ's Second Coming, then rupture and rapture are here endowed with a second possibility. The rupture is never only itself and neither is rapture; each is inextricably bound to the other.

As much as Pasolini's self is helpful for thinking a different form of the self up to the challenges of this political and ethical moment of late capitalism, it remains too closely linked to a postlapsarian moment when the self remains caught up in the embrace of Jesus-the-Christ. The comic self understands the rupture of self-possession differently in a much more undisciplined fashion. The "real" self, for Pasolini, renews its commitment to "renounce" any form of its old self every day, or its old everyday self, for that matter. Indeed, Pasolini implicitly pronounces as inadequate the post-resurrection demands that the event makes, every day, on the Christian self.

Much here will depend upon how we understand "after." Key is what happens after Jesus-the-Christ walks out of the tomb, back into public life. The event of "after" occurs when none other than Mary Magdalene recognizes him after she finds his tomb empty. Interestingly, this is the very first "after" that Pasolini invokes and is the "after," as recorded in John's Gospel, where Jesus-the-Christ is mistaken for a gardener: "Woman, why are you weeping? Whom are you looking for?"[3] This imperious rebuke displays an impatience with her for having doubted his return and rebirth into eternal life. It forms a politically dramatic "after" that stands as the unimpeachable example for how to grasp, in everyday life, and death, the "real." To become, as Paul writes, "imitators of the churches of God in Christ," it is necessary to see what one has failed to see.[4]

It is in the spirit of John that Pasolini raises self-renunciation to the sine non qua of the political self. Pasolini advocates and agitates for a form of Christian practice that arguably has only one precedent in Christian doctrine. It is not the only moment that the call for work achieves a such prominence, but it obtains in the Gospel of James as its singular focus. What marks James's Gospel is his call for faith through works: "Be doers of the word, and not merely hearers who deceive themselves"—or, offered in Pasolini's variation, work.[5] Work, plain, unadorned, apparently an ordinary activity but a mode of everyday being that is intensely "real."

A caution is needed. Because Pasolini so elevates the "after," it achieves the status of a calling that only few can answer; no less a New Testament personage than Mary Magdalene is found wanting. In her defense, she is made doubtful by mourning, but she becomes an object lesson in how difficult the work of "after" really is. When it assumes the form of Pasolini's Christian self, work is difficult. It is required because the rupture—to disarticulate the I from mine—involves the daily act of renouncing yesterday in order to do the work that today demands. Giving a comic account of the self disrupts the unreflective way in which possession has made itself historically ubiquitous, in the way that I stands unruptured in relation to mine. In doing so, the I continually forgets the rapture that is born out of the rupturing of this world from another.

The Time of Refusal

> We are punished for our refusals.
> —OSCAR WILDE, *The Picture of Dorian Gray*

To renounce is to undertake the act of relinquishing, abandoning, repudiating, or sacrificing something or someone. This is decidedly not how Jesus-the-Christ figures in the New Testament where he is a sacrificial lamb. Refusal instead involves declining, denying. The disciple Peter, in the Garden of Gethsemane, denies knowing Jesus-the-Christ three times "before the cock crows." To refuse as Peter does would, in our terms, require maintaining an interval between I and mine.

Exhibit A of the comic self. Refusal is not to give up (that would be renunciation) but to insist instead on the rupture that keeps I distinct from mine. So conceived, refusal marks both space and time: space, in that it keeps I apart from mine, and time, insofar as the time of the I and the time of the mine is iterable only as succession and never as singularity. I and mine can be spoken only one after the other, never as One.[6] I and mine do not conflate into a singularity. I and mine, in their succession, point to the dispossession of one from the other.

In the relationship that is I-mine, the potential for conflict is clear. We can name this conflict the struggle for primacy in the order of succession (say, "I always comes before mine" or "There can be no I without mine"). It reveals itself again and again to be founded upon the refusal to live by the terms of the other's refusal. I will not withhold its claim that it precedes mine and it refuses to cede its oneness with mine. We are not far from Derrida's notion of autoimmunity that reveals the time of refusal as subject to its own undoing because it seeks, at once, to proclaim its singularity and its temporal primacy.[7] The difficulty is that I and mine refuse to cede their primacy. Out of this refusal to accept relegation emerges their solid form. Neither divinities nor Olympian gods but robust entities, each is intent on securing and maintaining itself as distinct, sovereign, even.

To withhold is to exercise the right to keep apart, to hold separately, each in their own time and space. It is an ontological and conceptual space in which I and mine vie for power, each recognizing themselves in each other and thereby mutually reinscribing and reinforcing the other.

Like any "solid form," I and mine need reinforcement and, as ontological irony would have it, nothing reinforces the I like mine, or mine like I. Indeed, each depends upon the other for their conceptual integrity. Is this not just a perverse rendering of Oscar Wilde's notion of "punishment" that concludes *The Picture of Dorian Gray* such that the separation of I from mine operates as purification? Is refusal an explicit acknowledgment of the shared precariousness and love each bears the other that would, were it not for the comic self, bind I to mine? Punishment follows refusal because refusal acts punitively against love. That "solid form"—exactly how "solid" are I and mine? Solid enough to refuse the emergence of the individual? Yes. Solid enough to provide prophylaxis against the promise of love, which the I is so capable of demonstrating in relation to that which it deems mine? Yes.

Where the contemporary self experiences the promise of the continual enmeshment of I and mine under the cover of love and calls it individuation (or not), the comic self accents a holding apart. It remains faithful to the logic of the rupture that refuses any contraction of mine into I. Its refusal pertains to how the comic self maintains itself in a state of dispossession, dissenting from the expansion of I or the logic of possession into a selfhood that is able to draw the rupturous I or the rupturous mine into its orbit. As unsettling as this may be to contemporary life, the comic self disallows any expansion into singularity.

Admittedly, to militate against expansion is to recognize that an element of the disciplinary hangs about the comic self. And yet this is understandable given that discipline is required to maintain rupture when faced with the threat of contraction. The rupturous reveals the ways in which contraction and expansion both depend upon the act, and the art, of drawing the other into something that is other than possession but that maintains proximity.

Against such a propensity for possession stands the comic self, actively poised to refuse, if we take "refuse" here as a form of resistance, the work of acquisition that possession requires. Without this work, there can be no contraction—a reduction into a One that does not translate into a One that is necessarily smaller—or an expansion—making out of the One a larger One, maybe even a more capacious, accommodating

One. Elision precedes contraction but contraction cannot erase the traces, the Derridean spur, of elision. Neither contraction nor expansion can omit entirely the remainder effected by elision.[8]

What are the effects of refusing to possess? The principal one is "passive" in Georges Sorel's sense insofar as it, like the striking worker and his "ethic of the political sect," keeps itself absolutely apart from any and all outsiders.[9] Refusal names the political work of keeping separate, of I-removal and mine-removal, by militating against contraction or, rendered in a more obviously political register, the consolidation of forces.[10] Rupturous by nature, the comic self affirms alienation, Marx's concept that finds a stringent, unbending, separatist resonance in Sorel's hands. The comic self stands as the I that affirms its alienation from mine, a declaration met, word for word, intensity for intensity, in like refusal by mine. This is a mine that refuses the subject that possesses and an I that refuses the means of possession, a figure without head and without hands.

A "Shapeless Mist"

It is a particular kind of work, maintaining the rupture that permits the quality of rapturousness to hold sway in the comic self. By refusing all inclination toward contraction and expansion, the comic self puts paid to the event of the self as the consequence of, as the verisimilitude that is, I-mine. Writing on the difference between male ("Mr. A") and female ("Mary Carmichael") in *A Room of One's Own,* Virginia Woolf reflects on how the contraction that is I also works as an exclusionary force. The force of exclusion is such that, for Woolf, it obliterates what surrounds it, putting everything else in what she names the "shadow," insuperable, effectively blocking out everything but itself, the overwhelming I:

> But after reading a chapter or two a shadow seemed to lie across the page. It was a straight dark bar shaped something like the letter "I." One began dodging this way and that to catch a glimpse of the landscape behind it. Whether it was a tree or a woman walking I was not quite sure. Back one was always hailed to the letter "I." One began to be tired of "I." Not but what this "I" was a most respectable "I" honest and logical; as hard as a nut, and polished for centuries by good teaching and good feeding. I respect and admire that "I" from the

bottom of my heart. But here I turned a page or two, looking for something or other the worst of it is that in the shadow of the letter "I" all is shapeless mist. Is that a tree? No, it is a woman.[11]

Much like Woolf, we are bound by "centuries [of] good teaching" to "respect and admire that 'I,'" although our respect and admiration may leave, at least in relation to hers, something to be desired. However, unlike Woolf, it is not so much the "shadow" that preoccupies us. After all, in *A Room of One's Own,* Woolf clears away the "shapeless mist" in order that the "woman," the novelist, sustained by £500 and her own room, might come fully into view; a "shapeless mist" that has, of course, enshrouded and obscured several potential novelists, to say nothing of the other talents, propensities, and desires that have been thwarted. The "I," male, writer (of fiction and much else besides), white, and seemingly indomitable, condemns everything that does not conform to this profile of "I" to a Woolfian "shadow." The "shadow knows," and there is nothing even remotely pleasant about what this "shadow knows." Anti-essentialist, relentlessly materialist, and adamantly opposed to the fiction of the starving artist (every writer deserves a good meal every evening), *A Room of One's Own* sketches for us an "I" that incarnates the logic of possession. Everything that "I" does not possess is not worthy of possession and, as such, must be cast into the "shadow."[12]

Whether by default or not, a beneficiary of a patriarchal and a particular racial order, Woolf presents to us an "I" that is unthinking in its selfhood or in its immovable "I-ness." This "I" has contracted mine into "I" so thoroughly as to make the very possibility of mine entirely superfluous in its possession of the "I." Woolf's is the "I" in extremis. It appropriates, consuming all before it without so much as an afterthought for those that have been exiled to the "shadows." A vast expanse of historical time separates Woolf's "I" from all who lurk, most likely against their wishes, in the "shadows."

The determination to secure for women writers "a room of their own" coincides with the comic self in their shared refusal to abide the all-consuming "I." Woolf works to move her "I" (a figuring of the self that has no room for her) from its position of historical superimposition that derives from, dialectically, a history of subjugation and exclusion.

The comic self, in its turn, is intent on emerging from being possessed by Woolf's "shadow" in order to dispossess her "I." If *A Room of One's Own* is a work redolent with pithy irony, the comic self is preoccupied with how to dispossess. Woolf wants to rearrange, in significant measure, the stage on which her "I" with its distinctly racialized and heteronormativized profile has, to date, felt free to dominate. The comic self also holds the "I" up for scrutiny but is intent on breaking Woolf's "I" in two. It wants to snap the "straight dark bar" in half, in order that it might never be reset into such unbreakability again. To do so, it begins from the premise that the "shapeless mist" is precisely what militates against the demystification of Woolf's "I." In fact, the effect of this "shapeless mist" is to hold everything in "shadow," the "hard as a nut" "I" more than anything else. Dispossessing the "I," subjecting it to rupturousness, is the only way to "turn the page" on this formidable figure and to bring into view the fold, so Leibnizian in its history and architecture, that binds I to mine.

The comic self is "looking for that something" that goes unspoken by Woolf. It wants to clear the "mist" because it is not so much "tired of 'I'" as it is impatient with the ongoing effects of possession. Woolf's is, of course, not a project geared toward dispossession, but it is a salient critique of "I's" unquestioned discursive and philosophical dominance. For its part, the comic self marks the unmooring of "I" from itself; it destabilizes "I," wrenching "I" out of the "shapeless mist" in order to reveal dispossession as the "I's" kryptonite. If Woolf's "I" is not afforded the right to possession-without-acknowledgment-of-possession, it shows itself to be, indeed, not the all-conquering figure of white masculinity it purports to be but, instead, an "I" that cannot sustain the possibility of dispossession. "I" without mine might very well be itself susceptible to being consumed into the "shapeless mist." Or alternately, Woolf's "I" might be consumed as a figure no more in possession of a "shape" than a "shapeless mist."

CHAPTER 3

Elide Tragedy

Elision is the linguistic and materialist antidote to the geomythology of self-possession. It strikes out the I from the mine, making it impossible for the self to speak of itself in terms of possession. It enjoys a profound relationship to the comic self because its negational force opens up a time and space for thinking against self-possession. A phenomenological term, elision is the means by which the comic self reveals the fallacy of self-possession, restoring I and mine in/to their rupture, dispossessing one from the other. Each is dispossessed of what it cannot possess, except when understood in the geomythology of self-possession.

Elision returns the meaning of the I and the mine from the ontic to the ontological in the figure of the comic self. Phenomenologically, the comic self exercises the principle of reduction and the art of contraction insofar as it extrapolates the I from the mine, contracting each into its reduced specific, intense form. Acting as crucible, the comic self liberates the I from its contraction into I-mine, and vice versa.

We spoke of *Julius Caesar* earlier on as the figure of anadiplosis, and so it is not surprising that we should turn to the play again in weighing the force of the comic self. In the 1970 film version of *Julius Caesar*, starring Charlton Heston, anadiplosis achieves an architectural viscerality.[1] Heston's Mark Antony, given permission by Brutus, ascends the steps and delivers his speech. As his oration begins to manifest its political impact,

Mark Antony descends, and with every step he takes, the crowd of com-mon people inches closer and closer to the conspirators. With each pass-ing step Mark Antony takes, the fear on Brutus's face increases (Brutus is played by Jason Robards). By the time that Heston holds Caesar's coffin, having ascended the steps to read the contents of Caesar's will, the crowd's menace is palpable. The contents of the will reveal Caesar's magnanimity, riling up the crowd: "To every Roman citizen he gives, / To every several man seventy-five drachmas."[2] Anadiplosis ruptures one descent (Mark Antony's) from the other (Brutus et al.).

Anadiplosis works literally and metaphorically. As Mark Antony de-scends, in a show of democratic force, since he is of the crowd, the self-same crowd that is now so menacing the conspirators, Caesar's political stock and Mark Antony's rise. They forget Caesar's transgressions and Brutus and Cassius, in double-quick time, go from saving the Republic to killing it. Caesar's ascent has been secured, at the expense of Brutus's and his fellow conspirators' descent (we note in passing the ethical indif-ference of the "pit"). No one knows this as well as Mark Antony, who at the end of the scene remarks to himself: "Now let it work. Mischief, thou art afoot. Take thou what course thou wilt."[3]

Anadiplosis is a dangerous political tool in the mouth of the agent provocateur; more dangerous still in the mouth of an agent provocateur who knows precisely the endgame and outcome of this "course" of action he has unleashed. It will be a spiral of violence that moves upward and downward, from the top (dignitaries) of the funeral dais to the bottom (public), from the bottom, out of the anger fomented by Mark Antony, to the top, where Brutus, Cassius, and their fellows find themselves vulner-able to the public's anger. Anadiplosis functions ambiguously, and so the work of the comic self is to make itself subject to the terrain even when volatile, not knowing the self but allowing itself to be affected by the spi-ral and to determine the most effective tactic in response.

After all, Caesar's lack of fortitude and even manliness emerges when he reveals himself a champion of the downtrodden: "When the poor have cried, Caesar hath wept: Ambition should be made of sterner stuff."[4] Moreover, Mark Antony, as Brutus and his coconspirators know only too well, is skilled in mobilizing the elliptical while reinstating it in a repe-tition that increases its negative force. In *Julius Caesar,* Mark Antony's verbal dexterity binds elliptical concerns, namely "ambition";[5] he can convert Caesar's imperial desire into populist beneficence, while at the same time he is able to reverse the conspirators' concern for the Republic into a sign of disloyalty of an especially venal variety: Brutus is an "honorable man." Mark Antony outmaneuvers Brutus because he understands the "desires of the pit," which begins and ends with the stability of the Republic, able to sustain either imperial ambition or democratic governance; or alternately, it is a "desire" that begins in democratic governance but shows itself not averse to the former.[6] The "desires of the pit" mark the populace as both fickle and vindictive, regardless of whom it has to sacrifice.

Let us employ Mark Antony's incendiary, politically devastating speech as our exemplar. If the comic self elides the relation of I to mine, then we might say that the tragic self operates elliptically, omitting the intervening terms between I and mine. Mark Antony's adroitly crafted poem of praise deliberately glosses over his friend Julius Caesar's imperial ambitions, omitting any reference to them as Caesar's own. In its place comes "my heart," "my friend." No ellipsis is free: someone or something always pays the grammatical price for the sin of omission. Invariably strategic, Mark Antony's ellipsis undoes Brutus and leads to his death. The sin of omission condemns Brutus, Cassius, and their fellow conspirators to death and, since the logic of ellipsis demands it, the sin of commission too. To commit to excluding what would undermine the narrative of a life is nothing other than commission taking refuge in the shadow of omission. Mark Antony—political tactician, rhetorical master of ceremonies, in command of all his faculties, every word timed to perfection, every nuance and inflection offered with just the right amount of understatement and intensity. It is disingenuity of the highest order to pretend that he is leaving things up to chance "what course thou wilt." With that declaration, we are convinced that the "desires of the pit" form the raw material of Mark Antony's triumph.

Antony's elliptical power functions through his repeated proclamation: again and again, five times in total, Antony proclaims Brutus an "honorable man," each time with greater power, until Brutus's honor is torn to shreds, destroyed with a political shrewdness unprecedented even in Shakespeare. At the same time, Caesar's ambition has also been laid to rest. The elliptical of the tragic self works by leaving out what is critical and what is critically missing. Buried, side by side, with Brutus's (and Cassius's) honor, we find Caesar's ambition. Thanks to the elliptical, Caesar is rehabilitated and his imperial ambition alloyed into a populist sympathy, a distaste for power ("thrice upon the Lupercal") and a colonialist's largesse ("He hath brought many captives to Rome/Whose ransoms did the general coffers fill").[7] The tragic duty bound, as Deleuze tells us, to contraction/expansion subjects even the elliptical to its possessive propensities, bringing to life what it should omit.

Shakespeare's Mark Antony cynically and expediently renders the tragic self, which is by no means an exception in the logic of contraction/expansion—the contraction that cannot but extend into expansion. The ontology of the tragic self is such that in order to possess, it must leave nothing unpossessed (since it believes that there is always something more to possess). It does not suffer dispossession, regardless of whether it might be better to strategically withhold the sin of omission that doubles, when correctly deployed, as a virtue. One or the other is the difference between Baldwinian "triumph" and "tragedy." The tragic self names the conspiratorial body that contracts around the death of Caesar's body, which expands to such a degree that it becomes a threat to the Republic. In a fitting historical irony, the conspirators become victims of Republican retribution, killed because of their contraction around that very body of Caesar's. If they had been able to see Caesar less as theirs, the logic of contraction and expansion leading to their deaths could have been avoided.

The comic self avoids this fate by holding out the prospect for transcending its own body. To do so, elision is key, and it begins at the moment when the I acknowledges that its expectations are linked to the fully possessive mine. To rupture requires knowing how deeply the self holds the expectations as its own, but it also means resisting the temptation of suture too. The comic self recognizes that its modus vivendi is dispossession because it breaks free of what Brutus and the other conspirators cannot see—namely, the inability to grasp the relation of contraction and expansion as tragic. In the rupture that cannot be "repaired," there is where we will find the comic self.

It is also where we will find the unthought. So much of the thinking that occurs today takes place under the sign of the tragic. Expectations about the self become the stuff on which the future is predicated and readied, where meeting the expectations of what will soon be mine is extended to my thinking, my thoughts. The comic self undoes the conjuncture when and where expectations and property are presumed to be one and the self-same. It begins by disrupting the possessive claim to self-possession. By uncoupling I from mine, thinking no longer will consist in the incessant expansion of what belongs to the self and the tiresome repetition in which contraction follows expansion: this will be my thought, this is the I that thinks this thought. When the comic self commits to uncoupling the thought from the I who thinks, thought is no longer tinged with the ambiguity of belonging. This is the first order of business: uncoupling frees thought from possession; thinking follows from nonpossession, when it has divested the self from laying any claim to mine.[8] Yes, the uncoupling can be rude. Being disabused almost always is, especially when it comes to self-possession.

The comic self warns us against all forms affirmative and negational of the possessive mode of address. These begin with those modes that, in one way or another, turn on that (not-so-simple) word mine. The word is simple, but the claim is absolute. Equally, the comic self is intolerant of negative claims made upon it, aspiration-through-negation, let us call it, that cannot shed its acquisitive disposition, not even in negation. Is there anything more certain today than how deeply the negative runs through acquisition? I am not this, I am not that, I am the least racist person in this room, I am not at all xenophobic, and so on. In fact, the comic self comes into its own through the self-dispossessive speaking that is audible in/as not mine. In one articulation after another, everything turns on mine, even when what is not mine is being disavowed. This gesture cannot but alert us to some form of desire for possession, even if it is the denial, the refusal, or, at best, the recognition of the capacity of the self to reverse possession. As the Cynic Crates puts it: "You don't know the capacity of the satchel. A quart of lupins and a free and easy existence."[9] It is into the articulation that is mine and not mine that the comic self inserts and voids itself. Everywhere the form of the comic self turns is the potential for mine to be voided.

In other words, the comic self provides different cues for individuals to relate to the self, not through an acquisitive disposition alone. We are speaking about something that is more on the order of an intense self-recognition, as though the self by first refusing and then rupturing itself into the discreteness of I and mine, or in the struggle between mine and not mine, is surprised and perturbed at what it has gotten itself into. To phrase this in the spirit of Freud's *Jokes and Their Relation to the Unconscious,* the joke is on the comic self. Just look what the comic self has done to itself. All that philosophical navel-gazing has led to this. The business of undoing itself can now begin.

The comic self appears to be philosophically glad of this self-undoing.[10] Philosophy begins, the comic self ventures, with a smile part wistful, part incipiently mischievous, in every self's rigorous undoing. It declares this as though it were mock-reciting "The Star-Spangled Banner": "To the rupture we go, rigorously." Let the undoing begin, at the "twilight's first gleaming," if you insist. Contrary to popular expectation, these are not "bombs bursting in air" but rather the sound of terror emanating from the province of the possessive. That sound is the tragic self shouting its fear at what the comic self is doing, dispossessing, "bursting" the illusion of I-mine. There is nothing the tragic self fears more than the truth that is dispossession.

CHAPTER 4

The Comic Self Is Not Comic

The tragic self is right to be afraid. When the comic self fashions itself as agent provocateur, a rabble-rouser with a sense of humor, a libertine taking liberties, a speaker of truth to power through the power of the joke, and so on, it rudely brings its form into confrontation with what it is not. Through this confrontation, the comic self is made to understand that despite the adjective, it is not the comic.[1] It is not concerned with making anyone laugh. It may, but the greater likelihood is that it will not.

While it is true that the comic self is eminently capable of stirring things up, work of that nature marks its unacknowledged limit: what if this rabble-rousing through a crude or pointed joke is all the comic self can do? It knows that playing agent provocateur is neither its first calling nor its first order of business; provocation for its own sake is not the comic self's calling card.

This question of utility and the sociopolitical role of the comic self marks the point of distinction since that is where the disaggregation of the comic self from the comic occurs. The comic's role is functional, its social and political possibilities clearly demarcated: the comic speaks a critical social truth. Every comic has a mode of address inflected with its own brand of humor, a sense of timing (good or bad, although a comic who is consistently hamstrung by bad timing will not survive very long, especially not professionally), its own especial array of targets, voiced with a particular political sensibility, modulated or not by a propensity for the following: the expletive (a lineage that runs from Richard Pryor through John Belushi to Eddie Murphy to Chris Rock to Dave Chappelle); a preference for subtlety (Stewart Lee); wicked, ironic intelligence (David Letterman, Stephen Colbert, Jon Stewart); a propensity for self-deprecation (Hannah Gadsby up until recently); or an affection for narrative (Bill Cosby; Ellen DeGeneres) that may seem, on the face of it, to run the risk of inoffensiveness. If there are many ways to tell a joke, then there are at least as many ways to be a comic. The role of the comic has long been and remains vital to the life of the demos. After all, this is a profession that we can trace from Aristophanes's *Clouds* (where Socrates is the subject of the playwright's wrath) to Dave Chappelle's *Sticks & Stones.*

Yet, the work of the comic also demands that we recognize how important raising the philosophical questions about Being itself is for it. The comic does this work, to be clear, as an embodied self. The status of the comic's body is never in any doubt or, if it is, it is only to return as a derivative of the unconscious. The comic self operates more inconsistently, demonstrating irony and a convenient "absentmindedness." If the comic's body is critical to how the comic performs its comedy and its art, the comic self is only sometimes aware that it possesses a body. Indeed, it is entirely capable of forgetting that it has a body, hence its absentmindedness and absent corporeality. If the comic's body is fundamental to its performance, and if the comic's body is the comic's instrument, then the body of the comic self is incidental.[2] Here we are reminded of a doubling-up, as it were, on Jean-Paul Sartre's alternate title for his play "The Condemned of Altona," "Winner Loses" ("Qui gagne perd"), where, thanks to chiasmus, "the loser also wins, which is the title of the UK edition."[3] The comic self is both thief and unwitting victim: a thief who steals its own body and a victim who is not even aware that it has stolen its own body. The body of the comic self appears so superfluous that it does not even know when it dispossesses itself of its own body. The comic self is so absentminded that it is entirely capable of unknowing self-dispossession.

If *Phaedrus* is the signal moment in Socratic disavowal of the body, if much of African American letters is an object lesson in how to be, how to ameliorate, say, the reality of impending death through humor and laughter, if anticolonial literature draws our attention to violence done to colonized societies, then we can understand the importance of the body as the self's first marking of itself in the world. The body begins to signify too in relation to how the comic speaks a relation to racism or gender-based discrimination or to, once more, class humiliation. It is the instrument through which the comic develops, trains, and refreshes our sociopolitical consciousness. Sometimes gallows humor is our term for it, or there is the concept offered by Georges Bataille, as erudite a philosopher of laughter as one could wish to encounter, to die laughing and, in so doing, to laugh at dying. Consider too the *Phaedrus* in which Socrates arguably comes closer to laughing in the face of death than anyone. We are reminded also of the "injunction," itself an expression of political will, that "we laugh to keep from crying," Langston Hughes's bittersweet description of black resilience in the face of America's founding structural racism.[4] Writing as we are in the moment of the Covid-19 pandemic, levity and political incision of the highest caliber mark the work of the comic.

Sarah Cooper's miming-ventriloquizing of Donald Trump's "medical advice" that Americans resort to disinfectants to combat the virus occupies some of the more brilliant work done by comics in a moment when it would seem that all we can do is "laugh to keep from crying."[5] Or maybe we should all simply "weep" as we take our place in the socially distanced collectivity where Caesar stands undifferentiated from the "crying poor." Cooper's body, female, raced (black), is, in its performative-mime-ventriloquizing "silence," the comic body as that political instrument through which white male power, itself a marker of verbally inarticulate power, is shown up as ridiculous. Where it presents itself day after day as unscientific, intellectually vacuous, adjectivally obese, and, last but by no means least, grammatically garbled, Cooper's comedy reveals the white male body in its not-knowingness, because it cannot command language or intelligence. It is, therefore, fit for nothing so much as to be held up for ridicule.

It turns out miming white male power can appear to be a remarkably easy thing to do, even if it is not. When considering the mime as comic, what we fail to comprehend is how the work of the mime (or, in Cooper's case, mime-ventriloquist), its eloquent word-forming wordlessness that reverberates audibly, induces in its audience an almost involuntary repetition. This is a speaking and (re)ventriloquizing that occurs along with Cooper's ventriloquizing Trump's speaking. Her ventriloquizing—mouthing, as it were—her speaking without/while speaking in time with Trump's voice, inclines toward the gestural language of a volubly silent truth—mouthed words formed, forming, slowly, in the mouth—so that it finds its measure in its constitutive untruth. The time of the mime is what marks truth from untruth. Cooper's present of mime time or mime-ventriloquist time stands in contradistinction to the untruth that is the original, first speaking. Through repetition and ventriloquizing the first speaking by utilizing distension, recalibration, delay—différance, in short—the comic self establishes truth as the antidote to untruth.

Out of untruth, truth; a perverse, historically necessary dialectic. Cooper's performance moves us out of untruth via the body. The intensification of performance that occurs when miming and ventriloquizing enables her to achieve a speaking out of the deep silence but never silencing that is ventriloquizing. Silence here resonates but never reaches the resolute. It is what reveals, especially as in Cooper's performance, what it is intended to conceal. The word silently formed is the word made most audible. There can be no comparing the audibility of the formed-but-unspoken word in its relation to the spoken word that will not favor the former. We hear what is formed and not what is actually pronounced, spoken. The mime-ventriloquist works according to the logic not so much of the deaf and hard of hearing as those who cannot see. The audibility of the words being mimed happens at the expense of the spoken word, which leads to a conclusion: the formed word can bear the truth but not the spoken one. In Cooper's mime-ventriloquy, the self's laughter at the performance—that is, at the words spoken—cannot be sustained. Laughter responds inadequately to the force of truth. Truth is, to echo and pun on Gilles Deleuze's logic, the difference that repetition reveals.[6]

In critiquing the relationship between mimēsis and alētheia (truth), Jacques Derrida turns in *Dissemination* for a moment to the mime. While, as we have noted, Cooper's performance works not only through repetition and miming but also ventriloquism, Derrida's critique nevertheless obtains. And this because of the ways in which Derrida's argument attends to the abstraction of representation, broadly conceived. Derrida writes:

> The mime does not imitate any actual thing or action, any reality that is already given in the world, existing before and outside his own sphere; he doesn't have to conform, with an eye toward verisimilitude, to some real or external model, to some nature, in the most belated sense of the word. But the relation of imitation and the value of adequation remain intact since it is still necessary to imitate, represent or "illustrate" the idea.[7]

Cooper is freed from the demand to present a "reality that is already given in the world" and from the particularities that make up "verisimilitude." She can mold or "imitate" as she wishes because to "conform" to the "actual thing or action" would already be to introduce a "reality" that is unreal. Consider, for example, political pronouncements on science that are so misguided as to be fatal if followed ("drink bleach"). In accentuating this unreal "reality," her mimed-ventriloquized repetition shows the "inadequation" of the preposterous "idea." Truth is performed by the comic self in a "belated," but not too late, "sense of the word." (Here we are in full agreement with what Bill Withers and Grover Washington told us all those years ago: "Good things might come to those who wait / Not to those who wait too late.")[8] Mimed-ventriloquized truth sets out to save the polis from whitening itself to death, whitening itself from the inside out, a process that begins either orally or intravenously. Strictly speaking, Cooper's is a performance of anadiplosis that demonstrates how the unreal can shock "reality" out of its unreal—"Do not drink bleach, it is not a vaccine against Covid-19"—into a truth in the time lag between the first articulation and its repetition. Cooper performs the work of the comic self, ensuring that "reality" does not "remain intact."

Repetition and Recollection

If, as Søren Kierkegaard argues in his distinction between recollection and repetition, it "takes courage to will repetition," we can be quite sure that his understanding of repetition does not extend to Cooper's miming-ventriloquizing performance.[9] Indeed, so much of what Cooper reveals of "willed repetition" involves the capacity of the comic self to turn "willed repetition" into an act entirely devoid of "courage." After all, does it really take that much courage not to drink bleach? We are, in this way, taking liberties with Kierkegaard. What is more, we are entirely at odds with the precision of his distinction. For Kierkegaard, repetition ranks higher since it is what makes us "profound human beings" because, as he says, "If God himself had not willed repetition, the world would not have come into existence."[10] Through repetition we are able to be in the world and to function, even if not always as "profound human beings."

Without repetition, different worlds cannot arise. Transformation of the self occurs through repetition with a difference. In the case of the comic self, an ambiguity around repetition in its relation to the self is realized. The reason will be found in the earlier relation we sketched with dispossession. The comic self knows where difference is localized thanks to this relation. The line of flight from possession to dispossession becomes visible because of the ambiguity that surrounds it. Ideas, thoughts, objects, bodies, affects can be possessed. The comic self throws into relief the very notion that the self is, in any given moment, reducible to joy, happiness, sadness, and so on. Indeed, does the I possess my feelings? Difference and ambiguity do more than make of possession, a priori, a question. Why does the I stake itself on possession? What is given up in the act of dispossession? Both are questions conceived in and animated by fear not of the unknown but of the very knowability and, indeed, the intimate terror out of which these questions originate.

While the difficulties that the comic self raises do not coincide with the issues that Kierkegaard addresses, the ways in which he aligns repetition with recollection casts both in a new light. For Kierkegaard, recollection begins with loss, and while it may not attain the lofty existential heights of repetition, it is still marked by a particular significance, even if Kierkegaard qualifies it. He declares that "recollecting is indeed eternity's flowing back into the present," before adding a rider: "that is, when this recollecting is sound."[11] However, even in performing a certain low level of epistemic violence to Kierkegaard, we uncover once more the difference between the comic and the comic self. Unlike the comic, who functions according to the logic of the pantomath, whose desire is underwritten by the presumption that everything can be known, the comic self knows that it cannot know everything. Bataille calls this the "desire to know everything" that one derives from the perverse impulse to immunize the self against "suffering."[12] Therein resides the definition of the pantomath. The pantomath names the self consumed by the "desire to know everything," not in order to know anything but to present its not-knowing as its immunization against the suffering of the other, all the while promising to save the other, medically, economically, socially.

Herein lies another difference between the comic self and the comic: the first knows what it does not know and the second dissembles its aversion to knowledge, casting its not-knowing as infallible all-knowing. The pantomath is so obtuse in its relationship to knowing and knowledge that it mistakes itself for a polymath. Indeed, to disguise not-knowing, the pantomath must name itself. It is, unsurprisingly, in the grip of grandiosity and hubris and, most importantly, is subject to the force and intensity of its own not-knowing. For this reason, it must be a "stable genius" or "a very stable genius."[13]

Cooper's mime-ventriloquization animates the comic self's attitude to the work of knowing, a mise-en-scène on the order of Derrida's "mimodrama."[14] This is a "drama" that only mimesis can procure for us, one that Cooper intensifies into a "mimovetrodrama." She performs what the lack of knowledge looks like and, by extension, how the comic self repeats what is alien but not unfamiliar to it, this advocacy for the consumption of "bleach" as a medical remedy, eminently knowable. Cooper's comic self is able to mobilize the attitude of not-knowing through the repetition of (white male) ignorance. How can the comic self, as in this extreme circumstance, repeat not-knowing into an attitude that reveals the human cost of willful ignorance while, at the same time, hold it apart from its mode of not-knowing? In Kierkegaardian terms, the blurring of the distinction between repetition and recollection marks Cooper's performance. Of course, it is reasonable to think that no human being needs to be reminded of the potential dangers of drinking bleach or, in the words of the British comedian Stewart Lee, "mainlining Dettol" (an antiseptic commonly used in Britain and many of its former colonies).[15] In Cooper's miming-ventriloquizing of Trump advocating the use of bleach, repetition takes on an entirely different aspect. On the one hand, repetition is an act in which the comic self chooses whether or not to repeat. On the other, it is also a moment in which the comic self is revealed as a subject of repetition. The comic self is saying what it has heard, while it simultaneously appears to be intoning what lies everywhere around it. If the consumption of bleach or Dettol is the zeitgeist (if it truly is), then repetition can be said to assume a life of its own that requires articulation and agency, while maintaining a stubborn independence from, and even indifference to, the comic self.

For repetition to work, recollection must fail. If the comic self has to remind itself not to consume a toxic substance, then the only way to break the cycle of repetition is through recollection. To remember science, to check our list of facts about toxic substances, or, if all else fails—since common sense clearly has—to retrieve a fear of death from our consciousness is necessary. On this matter, Stewart Lee remarks with a marvelousness born entirely of incredulity and a vain attempt to restore common sense: "It is worth remembering this. That which does not kill us makes us stronger, but that which does kill us actually does kill us. Dead!"[16] In his intensely obvious way, Lee reminds us about how Kierkegaard's concepts work. To think is to act is to repeat. To think is to repeat the comic self to such a degree that it does not act. Thinking is making possible a life-sustaining prohibition, to recollect from knowing the importance of not acting, and to draw on an understanding of the past, death by poisoning as the incentive to prohibit repetition. Simply phrased, to think is to remember what has killed us—"Dead!"—again. Repetition and recollection are linked as an ambiguity in the comic self, out of which emerges the possibility of a different outcome and perhaps a different world.

We are again riding roughshod over Kierkegaard's fine distinctions, but in doing so, we remind ourselves that, in moments such as "Cooperesque" performance, the distinction between the comic and the comic self is revealed as porous, made so by bleach, no doubt. Out of this permeability emerges the nuance and subtlety that obtains with carefully wrought Kierkegaardian distinction. This is a subtlety that produces not just laughter: how ridiculous is this President Pantomath who would not know a polymath from a pantomath and would be astounded to learn about how much of a Pollyanna he is.

From Comedy to Tragedy and Back

It may be helpful to extend Friedrich Nietzsche's critique of the myopic nature of the lyric poet in *The Birth of Tragedy* when distinguishing the comic and tragic selves. "Tragedy," Nietzsche writes, "shows how far the visionary world of the lyric poet can distance itself from that phenomenon clearly standing near at hand."[17] If it is through tragedy that the "lyric poet's" view of the world is expanded, then what the comic self presents is a focused, intense philosophical interrogation of the self. It is the self, and only the self, that is thought.

Funny or not, scandalous or reticent, Chris Rock or Hannah Gadsby, loud or wryly sardonic, Lenny Bruce or Doonesbury, our protagonist is founded on a relation to the other. It is for and toward the other that the comic reaches, inclining outward in the direction of that self that is not itself. With the comic, everything is mediated; the medium is the message. Even if the joke is on the comic (Chappelle's Clayton Bigsby, the world's only blind, black white supremacist), it is a joke mediated through retransmission. By the end of the joke, the comic finds itself in the position of being able to reevaluate the joke. The joke is thought in order that it might be rethought; comedy as circularity; comedy as the most hilarious iteration of Derrida's spur. The material contains within it the germ of old material and so the comic is never done with the joke, nor the joke with the comic. In other words, the joke inclines toward anadiplosis to the degree it picks a recent moment and repeats it.

The joke always returns to the comic. Chappelle's Clayton Bigsby skit opens with a disavowal of racism. The white "Frontline" TV show "spoofs" a *60 Minutes* interview, with the white interviewer, Chet Wallace (Mike Wallace with the voice and inflection of Lesley Stahl; Ed Bradley nowhere in sight), exhibiting, for a moment, racial sensitivity, restricting himself to abbreviation of the "N-word," as he so politely puts it. Then, in a rhetorical gesture more anaphora than anadiplosis, Chet Wallace pronounces the word in full. Chet Wallace does so with what can only be described as austere glee: "And by 'N-word' I mean 'Nigger.'"[18] Ending in anadiplosis, the spoof has Bigsby, now outed as black, telling Chet that he has filed for divorce and that he has decided to leave his white wife after nineteen years of marriage because said white wife is a "nigga lover."[19]

Anadiplosis, in the hands of the (African American) comic, explodes rhetorically, steering Clayton Bigsby toward his own self-destruction. A biblical inflection here shapes the deployment of anadiplosis in relation to his final decision. There are, borrowing from the Gospel of Matthew, none so blind as those who do not see, or will not, as the case might be, see.[20]

The joke returns on Clayton Bigsby, as it does for all comics, because the joke fulfills what Constantin Noica calls the "circle schema": a figure that always involves an unending interplay among thinking, knowledge, being, and Being.[21] In such a logic, the joke guarantees, no matter the circuitousness of the circular path, a return to itself: completing the circle, the comic reveals a path for the comic self. Magnitude matters little. What is key is the recognition that the comic almost always offers us something other than the comic itself.

That something is attitude. Comedy deterritorializes genre into attitude, and deterritorialized as attitude, it is again deterritorialized around the self. The effect of this is that when everything is comedy or when everything comes with pleasure, you can feel good about an outcome as extreme or apocalyptic as, say, the world ending. It becomes possible to delight or revel in the negativity of irony. On the one hand, this is the opposite of, say, that catchy refrain of R.E.M., the American masters of bleak irony and dark foreboding, often presented with a catchy beat or melancholy longing: "It's the end of the world as we know it and I feel fine."[22] On the other hand, the comic self is not ironic because it has wrested the self from the comic/tragic distinction. Out of this extraction, the comic self has made of comedy an ontological figure, and so we find ourselves returning to our point of origin—anadiplosis precedes us. The comic self follows deterritorialization.

This also means that the comic self can never be disarticulated from the comic. These acts of mutual possibility or inextricable entanglement suggest that when we think the comic or the comic self, we are always operating only at a single remove from its other. One is not necessarily constitutive of the other, but their proximity demands an account that will not permit of exclusivity or the sovereignty of either one or the other.

To phrase this in its most base form: if the comic traffics in jokes, then the comic self presents us with an entirely different order of philosophical seriousness—a seriousness, Jacques Lacan will say, that is missing on the order of "transference" that takes place between comic self and comic. As he says at the very beginning of his lectures on transference, "transference involves much more than the simple notion of a dissymmetry between subjects."[23] The comic self and the comic are linked through a "simple . . . dissymmetry," the lack of symmetry between (each other) that cannot undo or override the ways in which one recalls the other or the ways in which one resonates within the other. Moreover, the invocation of this "simple notion of a dissymmetry" touches on our question of the relation between the comic and self by introducing the unequal, a concept about which we will have more to say shortly.

Seriousness never denies itself the pleasure of a joke, except to bring things full circle: for the comic self, the joke occurs only at the beginning of the encounter with itself. The joke always begins again, and the end of the joke only names the beginning of the joke *a venir*. For the comic self, the joke marks the mode of entrée. This explains why the comic self rarely tarries long with the joke even as it persists within it. The point is to render the joke entirely unfamiliar to itself. The comic self makes the comic unheimlich through a process of defamiliarization.[24]

The philosophical violence that the comic self inflicts on the comic leaves the comic, to take certain liberties with Bruce Springsteen's poetry, "bruised and battered . . . unrecognizable to [it]self."[25] The encounter between the comic and the comic self may be conducted in good conscience, but such an encounter is equally capable of revealing the full weight of philosophical inquiry. In those encounters, it turns out to be no laughing matter for the comic.

In its dispossession and absentmindedness, the comic self bears a striking similarity to the comic who embodies the joke. If philosophy is the within-ness of Being, the innerhalbheit, to coin a neologism, of Being, then the comic self names the within-ness of Being and becoming at work in a process that may, or may not, go round and round but always does so within the smallest circumference. Anadiplosis operates here only within a delimited schema. The comic self forges the greatest intensity of intimacy between becoming and Being, leaving only the smallest fissure between becoming and Being. Under these circumstances, it is possible to imagine Noica's circle as more on the order of a short, direct line that both becoming and Being share. Being is always within becoming, as becoming is within Being. The comic self in this schema names the extant connection.

In contrast, the comic's circuit operates more along the lines of Noica's circle. If his circuit is a priori overdetermined (the point of return is known, the condition in principle of philosophy is the circle), the comic's differs only insofar as it short-circuits Noica's process. For the comic, little time elapses between the opening and closing of the circle; the comic's circuit is preordained, historically ordered, and entirely within the circuit. It operates on the contracted principle of self-other-self; the arc and trajectory of the joke is known beforehand. Even the comic's closed joke works through (re-)circulation. The relation is (S)self→←(O)other, in a cycle that always comes quickly full circle. As such, it "closes" itself, folds comfortably, knowingly back into its mediated self.

For the comic self, things are different. Much like what gives Nietzsche "eternal pleasure," the cycle can be found in navel-gazing repetition.[26] Through narrowly focused repetition, the comic self is able to "miraculously turn his eyes and contemplate himself. Now he is simultaneously subject and object, all at once poet, actor, and spectator."[27] The comic self writes ("poet"), performs ("actor") and subjects ("spectator") itself to self-scrutiny. Its formula is, to coin a phrase, infinitely more enclosed and verges on the carceral. Best rendered as →CS←, out of which derives "eternal philosophical enjoyment," further proof of Nietzsche's sharp, self-reflecting sense of humor. Is the comic self to be taken as Nietzsche's law-and-order joke—that is, surround the joke and then incarcerate it with typography, →←? Knowing that it is already psychologically imprisoned, there is nothing left to do but keep the comic self tightly and typographically contained, on the page, anyway. What a thing this is to contemplate, especially if we follow Noica's designation of contemplation as "nostalgia for Being."[28]

This explains why the comic's intervention is philosophically inadequate. It turns on the presumption that the self understands its own nature solely for the purposes of knowledge. The very first gesture, the first principle, the constitutive ground of the comic self's philosophical standing, consists of an affirming negation: the affirmation of the negation of self-knowledge. The comic self knows that it does not know itself and so directly contradicts the first principle of philosophy: "Know thyself."

On this note, more than any other, the comic self takes its distance from the tragic, a rendering of the self that assuredly deserves its own study. As Hamlet makes clear, unlike the comic self, the tragic self claims the right to an I that it believes that it truly knows. The tragic self operates on the unfailing condition that what it knows is what there is to know. It understands itself as the infallible thinking self, working on the principle that it knows everything—everything worth knowing, that is. Its tragedy resides in its inability to see that the cause of the action is not the I's, despite all the faith in the infallibility of its thinking self. Indeed, all the major tragedies make this point amply: the conditions for tragedy do not originate in or with the I.

This is precisely what ails the tragic self. Overwhelmed by the notion of a self-possessing self, and sometimes even a self-prepossessing self, that cannot represent to itself the reasons for its actions, it searches for a raison d'être that will always escape it, that will always lie tantalizingly beyond its reach. The tragic self's raison d'être renders it unable to see that "reason" or the logic of the event lies far beyond its ambit, the power of its remit. Misguided in its nonexistent self-sufficiency, convinced that it can command the event, the tragic self is blind to the drama that makes visible, before its very eyes, its own lack. We know this as the condition against which Saint Matthew warns that there are none so blind as those who will not see. The mutual lack that constitute Othello (race) and Iago (innate ability, character) makes this blindness dialectically tragic in both. Each can only see the other's lack, and, in some measure or other, lack is tragically bounded by his tragic self. It is possessed, and here the term is glossed by the genre of horror stories and films by its own investment in utter and complete self-possession. The tragic self possesses itself, safe in the knowledge that it possesses everything that is worth possessing.

The comic self too suffers from a susceptibility to its own reasoning, which enables it to disown its own delimitations. And therein lies the rub. Instead of laying claim to its inveterate, infallible reason, the fallacy of absolute (potential) possession as the tragic self does, the comic self acknowledges insufficiency. By no means an unthinking or unreflective self, au contraire, it recognizes that there must surely be reasons for the action but acknowledges that these reasons are fundamentally unknowable. Because it works on the grounds of the recognition of the self's constitutive insufficiency, it is able to declare its lack without having to separate itself from any knowledge as such. Paradoxically, to acknowledge what is unknowable is, saliently, to know but not as negation: knowing as an awareness of what the self cannot know. This accounts for the comic self's openness to a future knowing, which then gives access to a retrospective knowing. Because the I knows, in either complete or scattershot form, what it does not know, it is able to construct the ground for a knowing to come. In this way, we can assert that the comic self is concerned less with truth so much as it is with an attitude toward knowing. The comic self, to oversimplify the condition, resists the possibility of becoming the victim of what is not (yet) known.

Is there anything more important today than to know what we know, than how we apprehend what it is we do not (yet) know? In this situation, each moment of knowing comes with an attitude toward the knowing. Again and again, what matters is our relationality to what we know. The comic self refuses to lay claim to or proclaim a relationship to knowledge as somehow prescient, omnipotent, and fixed. Our obsession with prescience and omnipotence interrupts and disrupts the possibility of our knowing what it is we do not know.

Laughter and Self-Owning

The comic's intervention names a hard, epistemological limit. The centerpiece of its representation derives from the incessant attempts to know the self as my own. The unsustainable and unshakable faith in the comic's ability to know itself always anchors this limit, since only this faith enables the comic to present itself before the world.

In the moment in which the repetition of mine occurs, the comic self stays ruthlessly alert to the repetition of this self-pronunciation. In its caustic response, the comic self produces the only sustainable and philosophically explicable response: it laughs at the sheer foolishness of the proposition of the self trying to own the self. Self-ownership? Who ever heard of such a thing? That's foolish, the comic self says, laughing repeatedly at every ridiculous attempt at self-possession. In command, barely, of its own idiom, the comic self is capable of constructing itself, in moments few and far between, in which the foolishness of believing that the self can be owned becomes clear. When that happens, the comic self finds new ways of expressing this recognition of foolishness.

It is able to do so because it ceases to express itself idiomatically. The sound of repressed laughter is Sancho Panza, muffling his mirth at Don Quijote's next quest for self-possession (and sometimes, as we know, Sancho Panza laughs outright at Don Quijote's quests). Self-possession is founded upon the affirmation of self that is also at once the founding of a self. The laughter grows louder because Don Quijote cannot even name himself! We recall that, prior to embarking on his adventures, Don Quijote was known, to family, friends, and his community, as Alonso Quixano, a noble or a gentleman "hidalgo" from La Mancha, a town on the plateau in central Spain.[29] Indeed, it is Sancho Panza who dubs him the "Knight of the Sad Face."[30] The joke is wasted on Don Quijote, though. In order to get the joke, he would have to begin from the premise that his quest is for the impossible: self-possession. Clearly, Sancho Panza is no Falstaff, since he cannot be shucked off by Don Quijote as Falstaff is when Hal has acquainted himself, in disguise, with Falstaff mediating, with the vulgus who are his subjects. Unlike Falstaff, Sancho Panza is indispensable.

What a price Sancho Panza, the comic self, pays for being indispensable! His role as the fall guy gives an immanent inflection to John Limon's repurposing of Freud's concept of "joke work."[31] While Limon finds "joke work" a way to describe the 1960s phenomenon of the urbanization of suburban-born Jewish comedians (Lenny Bruce, Mel Brooks, Carl Reiner, and so on), in *Don Quijote* Sancho Panza imbues the concept with a pronounced materiality. Not only is Sancho Panza expected to perform the burden of uncompensated "squirely" labor, he also repeatedly endures the "slings and arrows of outrageous fortune" that is the consequence of Don Quijote's recklessness and feckless pursuits.[32] However, Limon's critique of the "moral method of suburbia" and Sancho Panza's experientiality coincide in Lenny Bruce's and Don Quijote's ability to "trivialize all offenses."[33] Bruce is free to outrage bourgeois society; Don Quijote has no compunction about subjecting Sancho Panza to all manner of hardship and misery.

CHAPTER 5

"I Think"

We have been circling round a question in the preceding chapters and it is high time we ask it. Where does laughter come from? For Gilles Deleuze, its source is none other than Immanuel Kant's critique of Descartes's cogito ergo sum. According to Deleuze, Descartes's "I think" and "I am" fail to account for time, which assumes the "form of the determinable." "It is as though," Deleuze writes, "the I were fractured from one end to the other: fractured by the pure and empty form of time."[1] There is always a present—a moment, an instant—that stands between, to mix temporal and spatial metaphors, the inclination to "think" and the self who would be and who is doing the thinking. Into this time and space lurks the possibility of indecision; the inclination to think must guard, in the spirit of Martin Heidegger's *What Is Called Thinking?*, against the prospect of not-thinking. To incline toward thinking by no means guarantees the work of thinking. Anything but. As it happens, the comic self acts as both the instrument and the beneficiary of thinking.

The I and the mine can be divided into active and passive iterations of the self. In one scenario, it is possible to cast I as doing the thinking (active), while mine is reduced to the status of mere recipient of the I's thinking. Alternatively, it is the "mine's thinking" (let us name it, in the spirit of Kant, "my Idea") that, a priori, before all else, makes I possible. There can be no I without a prior mine that is a condition of possibility for it. While neither instance is entirely possession-proof, both throw the very notion of possession into question. As a result, the comic self ponders why I ever imagined itself to be indistinguishable from mine (anadiplosis, our own). Mine, of course, has exactly the same question; both questions emanate from the precarious position that is imminent dispossession. Just think of all the time between I and mine; just think of all the time it takes to get from mine to I; just think of how difficult it is to disarticulate I from mine. We are left to reflect on how all thinking is of time, even if all time is not the time of thinking.

Yet, the chiasmus of I and mine does not diminish the inclination of either to forswear the possibility of owning time. The dispossession that marks the comic self, beginning with the fracturing of the self into I and mine, reveals the laws of ownership as mere attempts to suture the fractured I across time by reinforcing mine over time. The I, as it were, makes claims upon itself, unsustainable claims but claims nonetheless, intended to redeem the mine for the I. Fallaciously, the I insists that it can be restored by making repeated claims upon what it understands to be mine. This amounts to nothing less than a claim upon time itself, which is made in the mistaken belief that the I can express itself as sovereign over time, if we recognize the double meaning and resonance as intended. We can render this hyperbolically as "I am time," or "I am time itself." As a universality, "I am of all Time."

Vertically, the I locates itself above time. The I seeks to impose itself upon time and it wants to make time subject to the I. Horizontally, the I understands itself to stretch, backward and forward, along an unbroken, endless line that reaches into an a priori past and infinitely into the future. In both directions the I persists simultaneously as the undifferentiated I and mine as either itself (I) or as an iteration of its self-possessed self (mine).

Étienne Balibar once again precedes us. He writes of John Locke:

> [He] thus separates two figures of difference, positing, on the one hand, uneasiness, the tension of self and own that maintains life and consciousness in a state of perpetual movement (which means uneasiness is the norm, that the normality of life is uneasy, troubled, or discontent); and on the other hand, the state of exception, or the limit-figure that arises when uneasiness merges with the monstrous, engendering a split between the corporeal and the mental, the radical dissociation of personality and individuality.[2]

In negotiating constantly between I and mine—here, Balibar's "self and own"—the comic self can thus be said to "maintain[] [its] life and consciousness in a state of perpetual movement," committed as it is to dispossession but drawn, despite and because of itself, toward possession. It must of necessity therefore conform to the "normality of life [as] uneasy." To be "uneasy" is to struggle with a "normality" that is anything but normal. To be "uneasy" is to think the "radical dissociation," the fallacy of self-possession, that produces "individuality," that iteration of self determinedly opposed to "engendering a split between the corporeal and the mental," a formation of self in which I and mine are, out of sheer habit, psychologically and linguistically contracted into each other. The comic self names a "monstrous" "state of exception" in which "difference" (in its Deleuzian articulation) works to maintain the gulf between possession and dispossession through the perpetual denormalization of uneasiness. And yet, normalizing uneasiness in no way precludes dispossession, which may explain why Balibar observes that a state of exception holds sway over the dissociation of personality and individuality.

The only "normality" that the comic self can abide is dispossession, when the "split" between I and mine is "dissociat[ed]," once and for all. This forms the comic self's "radical" core. Under this condition, dispossession reveals "identification [as] merely a postulate, if not an injunction."[3] To be liberated from the "injunction" into the "postulate" presents us with the work, albeit an incomplete project, of dispossession. To think in the time of the postulate is to be permitted to, admitted into, relentless, untrammeled speculation; to think in the time of the postulate is consciously and deliberately to open time against the prohibition that is the injunction. The comic self is possible precisely because there is no injunction and so, having disposed of the injunction, it recognizes that there is absolutely nothing natural in the identification of self and own.

Suspending Time

Without time, "I think" always stands suspended. Thinking is suspended for the time it takes the presupposed I to find its "occupant" (that I who "is," "I am"). Phrased differently, thinking is suspended for the time it takes for thinking to, as it were, find its "occupation" that registers an a priori mode and moment. The work of thinking requires preparation for

thinking that might be named "preoccupation": the time before thinking
that is simultaneously the time of thinking if not about, and not quite of
(yet), then for thinking. This might also be conceived as the time of inclination, preparing to incline toward thinking. Preoccupation names the
attitude that prepares us to think because we have been concerned about,
and not in Heidegger's negative temporal sense, thinking. The premise
that we do not know what thinking is, but we know when we are not
thinking, saturates the lectures that constitute *What Is Called Thinking?*
As the foremost and least alienable form of labor, thinking is work impossible to undertake without the time it takes to construct, reductively
rendered, that simple sentence. Descartes never arrives at that formula-
tion: "I am thinking." It is only possible to say, "I am thinking," in what
Deleuze names the "present present."

We can write this because the I cannot be carried from the past to the
future across the present. I cannot think in the past because to do so requires a mine that appropriates the past as an object of action that the I
cannot make or replicate without employing mine. Here we recall Søren
Kierkegaard's definition of recollection, which begins in loss where mine
names the attempt to wrest a past I from an irrecuperable loss. The I is always reaching for the impossible mine, which it cannot possess. To wit: if
I am thinking about today and repeat the thought of yesterday, then later
today I will think "both" thoughts in the past present. If I think the same
thought tomorrow as I did today and yesterday, then I will think them
in the future present, where it is very likely that my "pain and my joy," as
David Hume would have it, will have inflected each and, in the process,
added a potentially unexpected dimension.[4] On the one hand, we could
call the process by which our first responses manifest themselves "wisdom"
or "insight." On the other, it might plummet us in another direction.

The acts above involve how to separate I from mine, and so they hold
the key to thinking in the present present. Indeed, the present present
immunizes against an unreconstructed Cartesianism. The situation in
which the act takes place is a thinking unaware of what it means to think
and so does not appreciate, let alone comprehend, how much of its mental activity fails to rise to the status of thinking. This mental activity is not
thinking as much as it is the I possessing thinking by appropriating it, the
mental activity, the act that is not thinking, as mine.

Contrast this to the act the comic self undertakes, who may or may not be thinking but is merely preparing itself to think, by thinking about thinking as Heidegger insists in *What Is Called Thinking?* The comic self separates thinking from mine by employing an attitude of acceptance around preoccupation. It has a knowledge of time in which it comprehends and accepts that I cannot be transported into the future or the past without possession. The comic self does not approach thinking unprepared; it is acutely aware the terrain it is traversing involves tactics.

David Hume
The Master Critic of Identity

With tactical precision, we have arrived at the crux of the matter. It is because I think those thoughts as mine that I allow myself to lay claim to them as "mine." Everything turns on the I's claim to possession. David Hume, the enduring master critic of identity as self-possession, has a grand old time pointing out the fallacy of this presupposition. In a spirit entirely mischievous, Hume declares that because we do not have "any idea of self," something else must be at work.

> It must be some one impression, but that gives rise to every real idea. But self or person is not any one impression, but that to which our several impressions and ideas are suppos'd to have a reference. If any impression gives rise to the idea of self, that impression must continue invariably the same, thro' the whole course of our lives; since self is suppos'd to exist after that manner. But there is no impression constant and invariable. Pain and pleasure, grief and joy, passions and sensation succeed each other, and never all exist at the same time.[1]

Hume does not dispute the reality of the path that leads from "some one impression" to the idea. Instead, he rejects, plainly and out of hand, the effect of this impression, that "self or person" can be restricted to a singularity, to one or any one impression. None of our "several impressions and ideas" have a stable, unitary reference. The effect of the impression may be an idea, but that idea, and with it the reference that attaches to the impression, is, at best, suppositional.

A fiction, necessary or not, but nothing other than a fiction because any presupposition of the self-same self over time cannot overcome its constitutive inconstancy. At its core, the impression lacks veracity and sustainability. It is, above all, the impression, a temporal marker of our pain that takes place in a moment distinct from that moment in which we experience pleasure; our joy and our grief are hardly likely to be commensurate. It follows that if our impressions are not "constant and invariable," then no stable referent named "self" is available to thought, to be thought. Following Hume, all claims to self-possession must herewith be abandoned and refused the designation of "idea." Here, temporality is established as the phenomenological force that determines the irruption of the impression. The impression, say, of passion derives its sovereignty from time, and so commands its own time, even if it cannot be said to exercise command over time as such. In this way, we can say that each and every impression enjoys the sovereignty of its own moment, refusing to share its sovereign moment with any other competing impression.[2] The moment unto itself, this is the rule of sovereignty of the impression. Like Hume, the comic self laughs at the blatant incongruity between the articulation and desires of the self and the reality of those aims. Foremost among these articulations is the claim to self-knowing. It would also include the claim to the constancy of self over time, a claim that cannot but be grounded in the ascription to a foundational, unchanging, and, implicitly, unchangeable, essential self. For Hume, this presupposition registers as a "manifest absurdity."[3]

The best that can be hoped for is to know the "self or person" in its impressionistic moment. Hume, however, goes further:

> For my part, when I enter most intimately into what I call myself, I always stumble on some particular perception or other, of heat or cold, light or shade, love or hatred, pain or pleasure. I never can catch myself at any time without a perception, and never can observe any thing but the perception. If any one, upon serious and unprejudic'd reflection thinks he has a different notion of himself, I must confess I can reason no longer with him. All I can allow him is, that he

may be in the right as well as I, and that we are essentially different in this particular. He may, perhaps, perceive something simple and continu'd, which he
calls himself; tho' I am certain there is no such principle in me.[4]

Hume's intimacy with himself involves a pratfall, a bumbling, a reaching
for and toward that which does not exist, that self that he calls himself
"self." In part because he disavows the possibility of "simple and continu'd" self, denying that he possesses any "such principle," Hume delights
in this. In other words, only a fool clings to his perceptions; only a fool
on the order of a Don Quijote would be able to find an unchanged, unchanging self.

"Feigned Alienation"

An unchanging self that makes the comic self laugh? Slapstick will do it,
but forgetfulness will too. Consider those pages from Henri Bergson's
Laughter in which Don Quijote steps into the spotlight. In Bergson's
reading, Don Quijote offers a distinction between the fool and what he
presents as "absentmindedness," both conditions over which the specter
of madness hovers. For Michel Foucault, this is madness as a clinical impossibility: the ability to determine, with any certainty, the difference
"between feigned and authentic alienation," especially on that occasion
when "real madness and dementia [exist] side by side," revealing only the
"chimera of unreason."[5] Of all the terms that Foucault offers here, it is
real madness that occupies us most in relation to Bergson because of the
ways in which *Laughter* refracts Don Quijote's condition through a specifically Foucauldian lens.

   As our occasional comic self, Don Quijote shows that he is eminently
capable of overcoming his alienation from his "real madness." This pro-
vokes, of necessity, the question of whether he feigns his alienation, his
"madness," and if so, how much. He offers a negative instance of "feigned
alienation"—"negative" because instead of pretending to be alienated, it
is the moment in which Don Quijote is no longer alienated that raises the
question as to the extent of his remove from what is "real."

   This situation takes place in the presence of an esteemed dinner company. While the company is elevated, the venue is a lowly roadside inn.

The juxtaposition between Don Quijote's madness and his nonalienation sharpens, following as they do in quick succession. Just before he sits down to dinner, Don Quijote produces another of his knight-errant episodes. This time, while asleep, he "punctures" the innkeeper's "wineskins," proclaiming it to be the head of a giant, confirmed by the large flow of red wine that he mistakes for blood.[6] Almost immediately thereafter, Don Quijote impresses his audience with a proto-Gramscian "curious discourse" on the difference between "arms and learning."[7]

Delivering his "curious discourse" with erudition and insight, fully in command of his faculties, Don Quijote shocks his audience entirely. They go from having laughed at his "wineskin" antics to solemn admiration:

> Don Quijote had been speaking so logically and eloquently that, to this point, no one could possibly have thought him addled; indeed, since most of those who heard him were gentlemen, who quite naturally bear arms, they listened with genuine pleasure.[8]

It would appear, for a moment at least, that Don Quijote is able to overcome his madness. He can push the "madman" aside, though never for long; in its place is "a dissertation delivered so 'eloquently'" that his fellow guests are left aghast. For the duration of the dissertation, Don Quijote's manner is that befitting a learned man, a man unrecognizable from the wineskin-slashing "Knight of the Rueful Countenance."

Because of his discourse, Don Quijote gives us cause for pause. If the comic self is capable of feigned alienation, Don Quijote would suggest that the process works equally well in reverse: from "feigned" to engaged (his companions "listened to him with genuine pleasure") and from "alienated" to commanding the room. If the fallacy of the tragic self lies in the presumption that it knows itself as its own cause, then Don Quijote, in his ability to occasionally move between "madness" and "reality," can be said to perform a rare intellectual feat. He puts his "hearers" in doubt as to how stable these categories are, so much so that the "gentlemen" and the few women present have no viable means of reconciling "madness" to "reality," "alienation" to full and admired social integration. The comic and tragic selves abut each other, osmotically.

The precarity of what is pronounced as "feigned" reveals an effect of this irruption of the "real" in the figure of Don Quijote himself, a man of books but also a man of the Book, a self-proclaimed Christian, and a scholar of truth. Another is to recognize that "all men [sic] are intellectuals" and that every moment depends upon the capacity of all to think. The respectful response afforded Don Quijote after his discourse suggests that in order to think, the hearers must, for the duration that is the delivery, cease laughing.

Whether or not his hearers laugh, however, Don Quijote's dinner discourse has the effect of making all who hear him uneasy. The problem of the exception may very well be that it proves the rule, but what follows from the exception is that, if only for a moment, it destabilizes the rule.

Don Quijote will return to his knight-errant form, but his return will not quell the sly interrogative that has now attached itself to his representation as a man driven to knight-errantry by "madness." When "feigned alienation" can no longer be reliably deemed "feigned alienation," then all who are within the orbit of its effects are made uneasy, an effect of the intimacy that obtains between the tragic and comic selves.

Bergson

Bergson both produces a critique of Don Quijote that amplifies the physicality that the comic self assigns to Hume and provides a counterpoint to the notion of the fool. Instead of the "fool," Bergson proposes what he names "absentmindedness," only to undo that notion in order to lead us to a more profound insight.[9] Building his argument patiently, Bergson enjoins us to reflect on the effects of repetition:

> Suppose a man has taken to reading nothing but romances of love and chivalry. Attracted and fascinated by his heroes, his thought and intentions gradually turn more and more towards them, till one fine day we find him walking among us like a somnambulist. His actions are distractions. They are no longer cases of absence of mind, pure and simple; they find their explanation in the presence of the individual in quite definite, though imaginary, surroundings. Doubtless a fall is always a fall, but it is one thing to tumble into a well because you were looking anywhere but in front of you, it is quite another thing to fall into it because you were intent upon a star. It was certainly a star at which Don Quixote was gazing. How profound is the comic element in the over-romantic, Utopian bent of mind![10]

An awareness of one's physical surroundings keys Bergson's understanding of how laughter works; in this spirit he can excuse any "absence of mind." However, "a fall" is no longer "always [and only] a fall" when de rigueur behavior such as "looking . . . in front of you" has been unlearned in the cause of the "over-romantic [and] Utopian." This is not, as Bergson intuits, "absentmindedness" as such but an entirely new frame of mind. Don Quijote walks among the villagers of La Mancha like a "somnambulist." He goes about his life in this fashion not because he is asleep but because his "alienation" from them, which might once have been "feigned" (and even that designation is questionable), has mutated or transformed itself into the authentic. Somnambulism, in the case of Don Quijote, names nothing but the eventual effect of repetition, without a difference, the consequence of "reading nothing but romances of love and chivalry." When repeated reading of the genre produces a set of behaviors, repetition becomes a priori a mode of being in the world. Sooner or later, repetition culminates in something on the order of an automatic and automated response.[11] Lodged at the core of all forms of automation one finds not only a learned, programmatic set of actions but also the prospect of the robotic—what Bergson names the "easy automatism of acquired habits."[12] The robotic is understood here as the ability to, out of practice, out of the repetition that we designate "rote," secure a predictable, mechanized, outcome.[13] Bergson's metaphor of somnambulism is entirely apt.

The behavior is so rote that any and all actions it requires can be performed in one's sleep and, as the wineskin incident so amply demonstrates, it is possible to perform this action or function "in your sleep." So figured, Don Quijote sleepwalks through life, following the path set out by knight-errantry. The sleepwalker only emerges into waking when the tragic self is overcome, outwitted by the comic self. Only the comic self immunizes its tragic sibling against the fallacy that it is its own cause.

Phrased as a provocation rather than as a declarative, Don Quijote has made himself a spectacular, "foolish," and attention-grabbing victim to repetition. For this reason, he cannot be a tragic hero. Held in the thrall of the code that is knight-errantry, he cannot grasp how much the code possesses him. If we name mine as his adherence to the code, his embrace of the name Sancho Panza assigns him, and, above all, his fidelity to the

Book, then the key effect will be to leave him no choice but to insist that his quixotic I is utterly consistent with his mine. Knight-errantry can be, for Don Quijote, contracted into a single text: the truth of knight-errantry. Indeed, he belongs to the lowest order of monotheism: the Book for him demands no interpretation, to say nothing of the exegetical being completely antithetical to Don Quijote's (non)thinking. In its multiple singularity, the Book of knight-errantry is the truth, the way, and the life for Don Quijote.

The Ready-Made Frame

Bergson speaks to this issue in his delineation of "comic vice," in its difference from "tragic vice," as the imposition of constriction and mode of conceptual confinement. Bergson argues that the "vice capable of making us comic is that which is brought from without, like a ready-made frame into which we are to step. It lends us its own rigidity instead of borrowing from us our flexibility."[14] The "ready-made frame" is Don Quijote's Book, a program of action, a mode of life, which he follows rigidly and, it would seem, happily. He submits to the logic of the ready-made frame, which is indistinguishable here from the Law, because contained therein is τὸ νόημα τῆς ζωῆς, the meaning of life—or, as is more likely, ἡ ἰδία ἡ ζωή, life itself.

For the tragic self, which understands itself as its own cause, the rigid frame not only confines radically but amounts to an unbreakable construct. As such, it is an inviolable contract that binds the I and mine of the tragic self. Because it is its own cause, and because that cause owes everything to the rigid confines of the ready-made frame, the tragic self cannot allow that frame to be broken, since it would entirely destroy the very cause that grounds, justifies, and maintains the tragic self; it is the very reason for the tragic self's existence. It remains under the misapprehension that it is an omniscient narrator of sorts, that it not only knows but understands everything. In truth, the tragic self resembles the comic self, despite its repeated claims for how farsighted it is. Both are relentlessly preoccupied with the self. It cannot be otherwise, because the tragic self is so focused on the contracted self that is its own core. This is of a phenomenological piece with the ready-made frame that Bergson places at the core of the comic.

Despite these similarities, the comic self knows it is not its own cause. It knows that even if it does not understand. Its inability to command the rationale of its existence is met with an attitude of recognition. In other words, the comic self knows that it does not understand and, as such, is predisposed to looking beyond itself, adopting an almost laissez-faire attitude to its, well, desultory short-to-medium-sightedness. It can "see" what it knows, is aware of what it does not understand (or as aware as one can be of that which is beyond one's comprehension). This means, of course, that the comic self understands what it knows as much as it knows what it does not understand. None of this, however, should be taken to imply that the tragic self's interest is not piqued as to what lies beyond it, just beyond, or far beyond.[15]

The Book as Contagion

Don Quijote marks the generalization of a "certain rigidity of body, mind and character that society would still like to get rid of in order to obtain from its members the greatest possible degree of elasticity and sociability."[16] However, even if Don Quijote could be surpassed as a character type or a leitmotif, rendered comic in his "rigidity of body, mind and character," dismissed as a hidalgo overmatched by his humors, there remains the truth of his effect. The priest, who having overseen (together with the barber) the burning of Don Quijote's books, shows himself well-versed in the codes of chivalry, coming to the faithful-in-love Dorotea's aid as she stumbles in key moments, to say nothing of Don Quijote and Sancho Panza, who all step willingly into the rigid, ready-made frame. In crucial moments, Don Quijote stands as an index of the struggle between a society's desire for "elasticity and sociability" and the resilience, comfort, ease, and familiarity that is the ready-made frame. In Don Quijote, this conflict would, because of its ability to repeat itself so unreflexively in the actions of so many secondary characters, seem to favor the resilience of the ready-made frame. Repetition, then, is the marker not only of the automaton and the robotic, of the routinized, of interpellation, but also of dispersal across time, class strictures (the licentiate and the peasant farmer who is possessed of a keen political consciousness) and national geography, which extends from the plateau around Castilla–La Mancha in central Spain, around Toledo, roughly speaking, to Seville in the south and Barcelona in the east.

In light of this argument about resilience and dispersal, we cannot ignore the ways in which repetition functions through constriction and external imposition. On this point, Bergson is emphatic. Repetition begins, as it must end also, from without. That we internalize it, over time, does nothing to diminish the ongoing externality of action, the practiced, predictable series that is set into motion with that first act; a series that can only be concluded through the completion, again and again, of said act. In this figuring, the robot is the agent and what took place is repetition.

In his preference for the comic vice over its tragic counterpart, Bergson makes precisely this point. Spatialize the metaphor of constriction, Bergson argues. Somnambulism is naught but the effect of extreme overidentification, pathological attraction to, and fascination with the infallible heroes of an epic literature. Somnambulism, we might propose, is, finally, the achievement of an alienation of such an order that it completely obliterates any possible distinction between the feigned and the authentic. So much so that the law assumes, as it must in its response to such an individual, the name of Quixotic. In Don Quijote we have, in brief, a short and gallant history of madness. But, as Bergson reminds us, madness of such a stripe that it insists, always, upon its "comic element."

Except for very rare moments of, shall we name it, "reason," Don Quijote's is the world that demands that everything within it, from the most insignificant to the event—that is, every action, every speaking, every encounter—be "intent upon a star," since Don Quijote could not abide a world in which everything is not attuned to the logic of knight-errantry. That is where the human eye must be trained. It is not only, then, the comic element that is profound, but rather it is the profundity that manifests itself as the presence of mind to make such a reorientation of the world in, around, and far beyond La Mancha. Indeed, it extends to Persia, to Turkey, to Barbary, to whatever imaginary territory it is the Moors inhabit, to the coasts of Africa, east and west, Ethiopia and Guinea, to "Zulema's great slope"; it includes the historical conquest of the "Kingdom of Maynila," so as to make La Mancha unrecognizable to itself.[17] Such an absentmindedness installs in its place the presence of not only a new individual but a world completely reordered by nothing other than the written word. And yet, fantastical though the plot hatched by the licentiate to restore Don Quijote to sanity be, what the priest's coconspirators learn is that all roads, local and imperial, run through La Mancha.

This most unlikely band of conspirators comprise the local priest, Don Quijote's barber, Master Nicolás, Dorotea, cheated of marriage by Don Fernando, the driven-mad-by-the-loss-of-love Cardenio, also cheated out of love by the self-same Don Fernando, and, one regrets to say, his loyal squire, Sancho Panza. They are brought together by chance encounters. First, Sancho Panza runs into the priest and the barber, who determined to retrieve Don Quijote from his remote, rugged mountain hangout, where he is besotted by his need to declare his love for Dulcinea. Second, in this attempt, these three come upon the two spurned lovers: in order, Cardenio, followed by Dorotea. The mountain is reserved for lost love or, in the case of Don Quijote, a love unknown to the love object, so that his declaration of love approximates something like comic relief.[18]

If Don Quijote's is a world ruled by (his) madness, then the reason for his lack of reason can be attributed as much to his predisposition as to literature.[19] We have in mind specifically the capacity of literature to outlive its moment of production, distribution, and representation. Furthermore, if Don Quijote and literature are the source of and spokesperson for this madness, then it is not his alone. The condition is generalized with the figure of Sancho Panza. In hatching his scheme to get Don Quijote back to his home and to his senses, the priest believes that he has discovered the extent of the contagion spread by Don Quijote. Indulging Sancho Panza's illusions of a future governorship, the "priest was astonished by his stupidity, and at seeing how caught up he was in his master's mad fantasies, for it was obvious that he really believed Don Quijote was going to be an emperor"[20] In Sancho Panza, we find that even those with the propensity for the comic self show themselves unable to hold apart the I and the prospective mine.[21]

Why is this the case? To find an answer, let us consider the shifting positionality of self more generally. In his discussion of "Nietzsche's analysis of sexual difference," Jacques Derrida elucidates not only the distinction between men and women but the positionality of giving and possession that occurs within "woman":

> Either, at times, woman is woman because she gives, because she gives herself, while the man for his part takes, possesses, indeed takes possession. Or, else, at other times, she is woman because, in giving, she is in fact giving herself for, is simulating, and consequently assuring the possessive mastery for her own self.[22]

On the one hand, Derrida contrasts woman's "giving" and "she gives herself" to man's appropriative nature—"the man for his part takes, possesses, indeed takes possession." Were this argument to hold, and it does not (the proposition is provisional), the comic self would be designated as "woman" because she eschews possession. Woman does not submit to the fallacy of self-possession, albeit in a mode that is self-sacrificial and so not consistent with the comic self. For its part, the tragic self, by dialectical default, is "man," driven by what would appear to be a powerful impulse not only to possess but to take possession. However, in retaining to herself "possessive mastery for her own self," woman seems to revel in ambiguity by turns self-sacrificial, submitting to man's appropriation, in others asserting her right to "giv[e] herself for" herself: the woman (self) who cannot be possessed, except if it is woman who possesses woman through self-mastery. Rather than counterposing tragic to comic selves, possession to dispossession, self-dispossession to patriarchal submission, woman inhabits and exceeds both categories of self. In repeating herself, Derrida's Nietzschean woman, unlike Cervantes's, not only lends new inflections to difference but simultaneously performs rupture and suture.

The ambiguity of Derrida's woman, her self-shape-shifting, finds its analogue in the drifting, uncertain claim to (self-)mastery that is Sancho Panza. If we are to understand Sancho Panza as a comic self, then his is a self that is not only inconstant but also vacillating and open to seduction by the promise of colonialist conquest. It is a self unscrupulous, as such, possessed as he is of a colonialist mindset. Once he realizes that he can exploit Dorotea's performance as the "'exalted Princess Micomicona, queen of the great kingdom of Micomicón of Ethiopia,'" Sancho Panza reveals himself as having crossed the line between feigned and authentic.[23] This is the exact moment in which the comic self, always entirely capable of undoing itself, undoes itself: when I can no longer be held apart from mine.

This leads to a number of provisional conclusions. First, the comic self refuses, as a first principle, any possibility of suture. All suture depends upon an extant, ineradicable difference. Part A, having been ruptured from Part B, or Part C, having always existed apart from Part D, is conciliated—that is, brought together through suture. Of course, suture cannot, much as it strains in that direction, ever achieve conciliation because the mark of all suture is, as is tautologically inarguable, the mark that is suture: the stitches that repair the wound are the ineradicable mark of suture. As for rupture, the comic self holds it in historic tension. It keeps rupture, accepts its responsibility for rupture, without claiming ownership. Indeed, its very self depends upon holding I apart, and distinct from, mine. In the case of Sancho Panza, his infidelity to the comic self may be nothing more than a rustic hick succumbing to colonialist desire, but surely given the different registers of suture operative through Don Quijote across the novel, and the number of beatings that Sancho Panza takes for his relation, their coinciding inclines in the direction of suture.

Such a critique undermines but cannot derogate the fidelity of Sancho Panza's struggle when it comes to rupture. Bergson's "comic element" affects all of the conspirators, the licentiate, and, not least of all, Dorotea. They step into the ready-made frame but cannot remain held there. It is from his absolute fidelity to the ready-made frame that Don Quijote derives his singularity joined to rigidity of choice or, more properly phrased, the choice for rigidity. Don Quijote lives his life in order to protect the integrity of the ready-made frame and to discredit everything that surrounds it and any critique that makes the case for rupture.

Recall what Maurice Merleau-Ponty saw as the possibility of a new expression in depersonalization. "There can be speech (and in the end personality)," he writes, "only for an I which contains the germ of a depersonalization."[24] It is the comic self who recognizes this possibility by adhering to the truth of the rupture, by refusing to (re)align, as if through the "easy automatism of acquired habits," I with mine.[25] "Depersonalization," in this case, names how the comic self holds the self at a distance, keeps it at bay, so that it is no longer possessed by this self-possessive self. Depersonalization is a funny business, in no small measure because it functions on the principle of unsettling the self out of which it speaks.

However, and this is where Merleau-Ponty's critique comes into its own in relation to the comic self, it is able to locate this force against the self within the most intimate molecule of the self: that "germ" lodged, universally unnoticed, by the self who is speaking—speaking itself, more likely than not. Speech, then, is constitutively autoimmune because every time the self opens its mouth it undertakes the work of depersonalizing itself, it distances itself from itself, it wrests, as it were, the comic self's I from its mine.

While the comic self is busy depersonalizing, the tragic self remains blind. It cannot identify the threshold between seeing and owning. It claims, out of long-established habit, the I it sees as, a priori, ad infinitum, mine. In so doing, the tragic self anoints itself the Saint Christopher of the self: it will assume responsibility for the entire weight of the self. It can see no option other than to carry the sins of language from this bank all the way to the far one. Once more, the tragic self is enthralled to suture. It carries the sins of language so that they might be transported to where they will be laid down.

The failure of the tragic self is epic, and this because of the force of suture, the short, taut, umbilical cord that yokes I to mine. Out of this unforgiving, unsustainable bond emerges a self that cannot but engage in a one-sided relation with itself. The tragic self is held prisoner by its, shall we say, germaphobia. It is pathologically afraid of the "germ" that cannot be obliterated, exorcised, eliminated, from speech; it is a victim of what resides in language. Germaphobia, then, is not the fear of contamination from without but rather an unspeakable dread of what cannot be dislodged (from) within. Immanently understood, the comic self is substance.

Perception

In his "stumbl[ing] on some particular perception or other," Hume compels us to pause at perception.[26] To recognize the truth that is perception is to know no choice but to stay with perception no matter how partial it is. Hume's critique attributes to perception nothing more than a fleeting quality, no matter its ubiquitous presence: "I can never catch myself at any time without a perception." The "perception," regardless of what it is, "heat or cold, light or shade, love or hatred, pain or pleasure," will pass, rapidly: "The mind is a kind of theatre, where several perceptions successively make their appearance; pass, re-pass, glide away, and mingle in an infinite variety of postures and situations."[27] Perceptions here one moment, gone the next, having "glided away" to who knows where and having mixed themselves beyond their singular recognition. Hume does all the philosophical violence he can to those who put any faith in perception. He makes it his work to interrupt the intimate moment—say, love—that is perception by, in quick succession, acknowledging it only to dismiss it out of hand barely a moment (a different perception) later.

Hume's mockery of anyone who would "perceive something [so] simple" as the continuation of a self resonates with nothing so much as simple-minded, as though anyone so deceived were deficient in their capacity to comprehend the most basic philosophical principles. He delights in his alienation from "he who calls himself self" because anyone who stakes such a claim is beyond "reason": "I can reason no longer with him."[28] Hume posits himself, and it is impossible to miss his cutting irony, as the reasonable person who will not reason with the person who lacks reason—that is, the madman. In this instance, said madman is defined as he who is unable to undertake "serious and unprejudiced reflection." How much more lacking in reason could such a being be? It is a kind of silliness, this insistence on the "simple and continu'd" self, that rivals Aristophanes's hiccups in the *Symposium*. Aristophanes is unable to take his turn in the discourse about Love because he had "such a bad case of the hiccups he'd probably stuffed himself again, though, of course, it could have been anything that making a speech was totally out of the question."[29] It fell, fittingly, to Eryximachus, the medical professional, to take Aristophanes's turn. A "simple and continu'd" self is entirely "out of the question." Such a self is worth no more than the "hiccup" of a gluttonous playwright—or who knows what other malady had befallen Aristophanes. After all, according to Aristodemus, "it could have been anything." A playwright so besotted with his own importance, so addled in his reason, that he would seek self-validation through the misperception of philosophy that is *Clouds*.

Where does this leave us at this moment in our reflections on the comic self? First, we recognize that in the present present "I am thinking" is freed from the ownership of thought as mine since there is no object of thinking that pronounces itself "mine." There is thinking and basta. The thought of every I is sui generis, and as such it is beyond, already in its being thought, the claim of the mine, and yet remains nothing but generic. Second, the difference between "I am thinking" and "cogito ergo sum" lies in the former's intention to disrupt the relation of I to thought by creating a space in which the thoughts happen to the I. This is a chiasmic space in which the thoughts that arise out of or that are thought do so without an apparatus of self that makes them belong or cohere or, for that matter, glom onto the I across past, present, and future. As a self grounded in non-self-possession, such a fidelity to (this) difference is what permits the comic self to know that the I is thinking. Third, the comic self who, supposing that there is what we might name "comic thinking," understands that any inclining toward thinking is worthy only of laughter. This comic self laughs at the foolhardiness of thinking, laughs at the thought that we are what we think: *Nos enim ea quae cogitmus.* What a perversion of joke work. At its movable center, the comic self's intention will be found in knowing the I as a thinking I desperately trying to make thoughts his or her own.

CHAPTER 7

Temporality contra Cogito Ergo Sum

Gilles Deleuze's insertion of temporality into the self's relation to thinking begins to undo René Descartes's *cogito ergo sum,* and Deleuze shows that the result does not have to be, inevitably, tragic. Laughter is also possible. As a result, we find ourselves at a conjuncture: "What the self has become unequal to is the unequal in itself," a space in which destruction appears to be everywhere. We think that this account ought to be conceived as a theory of the vagabond or the voyou, redeemed by its post-Nietzschean promise.[1] In a moment when the self must be formulaically rendered as a form utterly singular, understood as "= ≠," the "I which is fractured according to the order of time and the Self, which is divided according to the temporal series correspond and find a common descendant in the man without name, without family, without qualities, without self or I, the 'plebian' guardian of a secret, the already-Overman whose scattered members gravitate around the sublime image."[2] For Friedrich Nietzsche, the untimely is that "meditation" so set against the grain of the historical moment that the thinker imagines himself to be "injurious to it," determined only to find a "defect and a deficiency in it."[3] If this is true, then the comic self is not untimely but indeed is entirely out of time; not like Hamlet's "out of joint," but out of time in the Deleuzian sense, where the "sublime image" refers to the I's destruction. Instead, the comic self belongs to Deleuze's "third time" in which the future appears. This is the time, after the revolution, so to speak, to which Deleuze aspires because it is only then that difference and repetition find their synthesis.

As an outcast, the "already-Overman" is the philosophical figure who exercises Martin Heidegger so much in *What Is Called Thinking?*[4] We know that Heidegger's Nietzschean "superman" is not the leader of millenarian cult but the "man who passes over": Zarathustra, who, for "Nietzsche, is the bridge to the highest hope to the essential form of man so far. That bridge is for [Nietzsche] the 'deliverance from revenge.'"[5] As Nietzsche intuited and Deleuze and Heidegger each in their own way acknowledge, it is impossible to deny the Overman's promise of the salvific, as long as we understand it as the quality of being saved from practicing revenge.

The Overman has delivered himself from revenge because he no longer rummages through the past and future. The Overman, as we will see momentarily, lays claim neither to that which was nor that which will be. He does this when he recognizes the difference in kind between the present present and all other temporal intervals. In truth, it is all very odd: the I fractured in the present is the condition for taking up distance from past and future selves created by the extension of mine to objects. In its command of time, the fractured I may well be suggesting that the Overman is the genus of the comic self.

We think in the present present because it is then that the I thinks thoughts that it does not immediately lay claim to. Are thinking and possession mutually exclusive? Are all claims on the I's thinking made from some time other than the present present? We are not saying this just yet, but we can observe that if the comic self intimately knows the present present, then it also names the figure within which that most haunting of Deleuzian questions—"What is a thought which harms no one, neither thinkers nor anyone else?"—finds its greatest resonance.[6]

Is the only "thought which harms no one" the thought that does not belong to the I? Is it possible, on the basis that we can conceive of that "thought which harms no one," to propose that only one thought must be avoided at all costs? Is thinking endemically opposed to possession or, for that matter, is possession what thinking resists? The only "thought which harms no one, neither thinkers nor anyone else," is the one that thinks thinking. Can we venture that thinking is what ends possession? Is that why the "comic poet" Aristophanes of Plato's *Symposium* so rabidly dislikes Socrates? Because Socrates makes no claims upon what it is he knows?[7] Can we turn Deleuze's question, democratic to its core, completely on its head and propose a Socratic declarative in its stead?

A thought harms no one if this thought threatens everyone. Socrates, after all, was put to death not only because he threatened the morals of the Athenian youth but also because he confronted the young men of Athens with every kind of question, providing them, most notably in the case of Alcibiades, with the philosophical capacity to live. In *Clouds,* Aristophanes, mistakenly in relation to Socrates we insist, denounces this training as sophistry turned to nefarious ends. Moreover, the instructors in sophistry are presumably well remunerated for transmitting their skills in the dark arts. Aristophanes on this count spares no one. That place where the philosophers meet, Strepsiades condemns: "That is a house for Trickery for clever souls." The intention of which is to hone rhetorical showmanship rather than cultivate a desire for seeking truth through the discipline that is thinking: "These people train you, if you pay them money,/to win any argument, whether it's right or wrong."[8] Unscrupulous, according to Aristophanes, Socrates, and his ilk.

We know that Socrates refused payment, believing he had no choice. After all, he proclaimed repeatedly to Alcibiades and to Phaedrus (to name but two) that he was doing the work of the gods and it would have been wrong to expect or accept reward. Socrates too spared no one in any encounter. Hardly a shrinking violet, our first philosopher, Socrates argued that the "thought which harms no one" must be presented to everyone and that they must engage with that thought. In taking up this mantle, we might say that Socrates "harms" himself and no one else. Aristophanes testified against Socrates on this point and was happy to mock Socrates in death.

This image of Socrates taunted in death articulates the relation between the philosopher and the comic self. Socrates emblematizes the comic self to the extent that he takes up the mantle of allowing himself to come to harm in order to show others the degree to which their thinking does not belong to them. It is a harming that also animates the historic ways in which Socrates enacts self-dispossession for philosophy's sake and how fallacious it is even to make a claim on self-possession.

We will return to these considerations in a moment, but for now the lead-up to the dispossession of the self requires our attention. We recall how Strepsiades, at the end of *Clouds,* echoes the final indictment that Meletus had launched against Socrates as an atheist: "What lunacy! Damn, I must have been insane/to drop the gods because of Socrates!"[9] Strepsiades is a gullible man, his head turned this way and that by Pheidippides. He is impressionable to the imprecations of Worse Argument and susceptible to the wiles of Better Argument. Instead of "damning" Socrates through Strepsiades, Aristophanes shows the weakness of the prosecution's case. If the foolish Strepsiades is their best witness, then the prosecution reveals nothing so much as its own "lunacy!" It cannot bring a thinking witness to the stand, and one suspects that the gods would not mind at all to be relieved of a believer such as Strepsiades. Once more, it seems entirely possible that Socrates was able to prosecute his case for his special relationship to the gods even at the cost of his life. Dispossessed of his philosophical self, there must, nonetheless, have been a certain pleasure for Socrates in having Meletus, unwittingly, present him favorably to the gods. In death, as in life, Socrates enjoys the last laugh.

The comic self emerges out of the dispossession of the philosophical self. We could say that when the sacred ship returns from the island of Delos, condemning Socrates to die the next day, it is not only φιλοσοφία, the love of wisdom, that is born but the presaging of the advent of the comic self with one dispossession begetting another. In its more expansive moments, the comic self reaches for itself all the way back to the moment when the ship's arrival, after a month's delay, condemns Socrates to die.

The suspicion lurks that, his denseness notwithstanding, Strepsiades has, as it were, been played. In his final words, he chastises Socrates for "laughing at the gods."[10] There can be no doubt that Socrates is "laughing" all right, but he is not laughing "at" the gods but with them. The gods and Socrates have always known how to share their (secret) laugh.[11]

To be clear, we have a choice: comic self or comic poet. And we choose to side always with the comic self. The tragic death of Socrates teaches us that comic poets are not to be trusted. They inveigh for death and then, parasitically, write for death in celebration of their own grandiosity. Deleuze warns darkly against such tendencies. Speaking of the eternal return, he writes that "the selection occurs between two repetitions: those who repeat negatively and those who repeat identically," both of whom "will be eliminated in the time of the eternal return."[12] Because he wallows in negative repetition, Aristophanes does not militate against self-possession.[13] Indeed, seeking to appropriate deaths that are not theirs, comic poets risk self-elimination. Deleuze goes on: "The eternal return is only for the time third time: the time of the drama, after the comic and after the tragic (the drama is defined when the tragic becomes the comedy of the Overman")[14] The comic self is aligned with eternal return and not, once more, with the comic poets precisely because the latter are antithetical to any thinking of dispossession and trenchantly opposed to any degree of rupture.

Deleuze typically will link the question of eternal return to difference. In a memorable phrasing, he warns:

> Not only does eternal return not make everything return, it causes those who fail the test to perish. . . . The Negative does not return. The Identical does not return. The Same and the Similar, the Analogous and the Opposed, do not return. Only affirmation returns, in other words, the Different, the Dissimilar. Nothing which denies eternal return returns, neither the default nor the equal, only the excessive returns: how much distress before one extracts joy from such a selective affirmation?[15]

Deleuze is not simply listing the unreturning or the nonreturnable but cautioning as to the amount of labor required to think what will not return to extract joy. That is where we will we find difference. For the comic self, this is the struggle—namely, to keep itself distinct from that which is similar if not the same or analogous and opposed.

Knowing difference as the rarity that is affirmation holds the comic self apart from the tragic. Deleuze writes:

> Eternal return is not the effect of the Identical upon a world become similar, it is not an external order imposed upon the internal identity of the world and of chaos; on the contrary, the eternal return is the internal identity of the world and of chaos, the Chaosmos.[16]

The movement between perforation (that is, one set of elements of identity resonating in another) and the negation that establishes the "internal identity of the world"—here will be found the comic self. It is not the world of "Chaosmos," but it bears, directly, upon such a construction of the world. Not to think Chaosmos is to submit to the "thought which harms everyone." The "thought which harms everyone" is the thought that Socrates thinks more than any other: death or, better, learning to live in order to know how to die.

Chaosmos

At the end of *Phaedrus,* Socrates faces death. He has offered his prayers to Pan, seeking to reconcile his "external possessions" with "what is within." He takes leave not only of his friends but of himself. His final words are brief and fatalistic: "Let's be off."[17] For all its colloquial familiarity—is this not how we would enjoin a lover, a family member, a friend to take her or his leave of us?—the dramatic circumstances of this utterance cannot be lost on us. Socrates's brief salutation, Ας είναι μακριά (eínai makriá), signals his final and most enduring articulation of self-dispossession. After all, as much as he issues his invitation in the plural ("Let us," Let you and I, Let us all), Phaedrus will not be party to this departure and so the Socratic self ends in self-dispossession. This is how we receive Socrates: dispossessed from himself, taking "off" from himself, to sup with the gods.

The comic self will not locate itself within Chaosmos without making demands. It follows both Zarathustra and Hamlet in that it "feels its hour has not yet come." We are "capable" of walking, so to speak, but not yet quite ready for the journey ahead, but our very preparation for that "hour" marks the "frontiers of our knowledge, which separates our knowledge from our ignorance and transforms the one into the other."[18] We must distinguish Aristophanes from Socrates, Strepsiades from Meletus, the comic from the comic self, and, most importantly, understand the difficulty of transforming ignorance into knowledge.

The comic self knows the importance of time. Here is Deleuze fiercely defending the time of Nietzsche's eternal return:

How could the reader believe that Nietzsche, who was the greatest critic of these categories, implicated Everything, the Same, the Identical, the Similar, the Equal, the I and Self in the eternal return? How could it be believed that he understood the eternal return as a cycle, when he opposed "his" hypothesis to every cyclical hypothesis?[19]

Deleuze rejects all attempts to eradicate distinctions—that is, to flatten everything into an undifferentiated same. Time, as Rudyard Kipling would have it, does not "treat these impostors just the same."[20] The time of "Everything, the Same, the Similar, the Equal, the I and Self" is not coterminous. Much more important, however, is Deleuze's attack on those who would present "eternal return" as an equal inevitability. "Time," he writes, "must be understood and lived as out of joint and seen as a straight line which mercilessly eliminates those who would embark upon it, who come upon the scene but repeat only once and for all."[21] "Eternal return" is both "cyclical" and a "straight line" without "opposition."[22] So much for inevitability and an indistinct—that is, unthought—sameness, as well as the logic of eternal return as cyclical. Nothing returns unless it does so as difference, produced out of a distress-inducing labor. Not for nothing, then, is Deleuze's affirmation selective. Only that which submits to and undergoes the demands of time, the rigors of intellectual work (thinking), is willing to risk itself.

Why? The reason again concerns joy. Who is willing to face the possibility of failure, to perish, to give up everything? Only those who desire a chance at joy? Only those who understand that I and Self are not interchangeable terms can even hope to return. Difference can only be derived from understanding that I and Self are not homologous.

Both the comic self and the Overman are familiar with delimitation of the self's sovereignty. For the Overman to delimit is, as we already know, to forswear revenge, since in doing so the Overman evades repetition, or at least that form of repetition that seeks to repeat without exceeding itself into an affirmative selection. Reductively phrased, to "exceed" breaks the mold.

The comic self does so by changing its relation to thinking. Fractured, it learns to think differently by repeating differently. It notices when possession creeps into thinking and inadvertently negates the possibility that the self can be possessed by thinking. To see ourselves across past, present, and future requires the belief that, somehow, we possess them through a consistent I that links them. Unlike the I, the comic self sees them across the temporal divide around which they conglomerate. Phrased differently, to "exceed" is to reject the notion that the self is what it thinks and to know that you are not what you think. Indeed, to "exceed" names philosophical ambition itself: You are thinking but also you are thought.

CHAPTER 8

From a Terminal Walk to a Tightrope Walker

The connection between not taking revenge and philosophical thought in the figures of the Overman and the comic self merits further reflection. Consider on this score Zarathustra's magnetism, his charisma, and his clear-eyed conviction, which make him the "common descendant" of philosophy after Friedrich Nietzsche. Martin Heidegger knew this intimately, which is why he seizes on the same role for the Overman, because for him the "superman is the man who first leads the essential nature of existing man over into its truth, and so assumes that truth."[1] Once more, the Overman is both the bridge over the abyss and the figure capable of walking the tightrope in order to get to the other side. What lies on the other side of the abyss? The comic self's dispossession, ethics without eros be damned.

In his reading of Zarathustra, Heidegger gives Nietzsche's "superman" (Heidegger's term) a line of descent, charging him with a historical and philosophical responsibility: to emerge out of "existing man into its truth." This occurs notwithstanding our shortsightedness and blindness, our stubborn resistance, and the limited nature of our philosophical intuition, manteia, that is our capacity for prophetic anticipation. We must not lose sight of this: the superman is not yet truth for he holds within his grasp and in his being that which will guide him to truth through or over him and, consequently, over all beings.

Nietzsche's Overman and now Heidegger's superman share a number of characteristics with the comic self, most importantly the rejection of revenge. To remain in thrall to revenge is to, at best, delay the passage to truth since, at its worst, revenge forecloses entirely the possibility of truth or Sein (Being). The problem with revenge is that at its heart lies a constitutive inequality that is both temporal and political—temporal because the moment in which intervention is necessary, when the political moment presents itself, is already lost and so irrecoverable to revenge, and political as there can be an exacting from the perpetrator of what was taken, lost, or done violence to. Revenge belongs above all and exclusively to Mnemosyne. We do not wish to suggest that memory and remembrance matter only to the mother of the muses, although we do recognize the inequalities at the core of every act of revenge. How else does Zarathustra let go of any appetite for revenge? He acknowledges and, more importantly, is possessed of this knowledge of inequality. By acting in its spirit, Zarathustra shows a comic self that will not be possessed by either revenge or the rage that so often accompanies and shapes the acts of those intent on revenge. Sadly, we know that thinkers are often the target of revenge.

This accounts for Heidegger's definition of freedom as "deliverance from revenge" and his positing of the superman who has been liberated from the shackles of pre- and postwar German philosophy and political devastation.[2] Indeed, *What Is Called Thinking?* constitutes its own claim for philosophical freedom, in an intensely political rendering that liberates Heidegger and his compatriots from the possibility of revenge. In the wake of the Naziism, the Second World War, and Heidegger's implication in it, the text retains about it the air of Zarathustra, who interrupts any tendency for Mnemosyne. The injured or victimized I chooses not—if only for a solitary moment—to understand itself as indelibly affected by and indissociable from the injury done to what is, or was, more likely once mine. To cast this difficult issue flippantly, Heidegger makes the case for "do as I say and not as I do." He comes as close as he can to acknowledging this when, early in the very first lecture, he muses that "prevailing man has for centuries now acted too much and thought too little."[3] Ungenerously perhaps, he says: Thinkers of the world unite; you have nothing to lose but your capacity for action.

Against this conundrum, we can see why Heidegger asserts that philosophy and thinking are bound together in an unbreakable pact and how it grounds this particular text. "Philosophers are the thinkers par excellence," Heidegger asserts; "They are called thinkers precisely because thinking properly takes place in philosophy."[4] Heidegger's account is, as much as it is a thorough-going discussion on thinking, also a determination to regain, deliberately, the superman for thinking. As history has shown, such a reclamation project has proved difficult, no less for Heidegger than for adherents of Nietzsche (though admittedly easier for the latter, and not only because of his premature death).

Nietzsche's and Heidegger's figure of the thinker anticipates Gilles Deleuze's "self," his cyclical representations of eternal return and commitment to the excessive notwithstanding. Where Heidegger is unequal to the thinker he so venerates, Deleuze, in a much more pointed way, contracts the self as one "unequal to the unequal in itself." If what Heidegger writes for, with something approaching a fervent hope, is the "last man" who can serve as the bridge to Being, then Deleuze's self presents itself as a thinking of a very different order. What kind of self could emerge out of an unequal "unequal to the unequal in itself?" The question is crucial in our archaeology of the comic self since it helps us locate just how excessive the comic self is when it comes to disavowing possession.

Selving

Dispossession occurs when the I achieves the intuition that past and future selves contract because of the workings of mine. This process we name "selving." In the moment that the I is dispossessed of its mine or mines, what becomes clear to the I is that the mine/s have escaped and, in so having departed, the unequal emerges. By "the unequal" we mean essentially this: the incompatibility and incommensurability of the self with the act of possessing itself. Consider a counterexample, one that Emmanuel Levinas proposes. In *Totality and Infinity,* Levinas insists on retaining the "universality of the same identifying itself in the alterity of objects thought and despite the opposition of self to self."[5] What Levinas resists, this in spite of his explicit acknowledgment that an "opposition" obtains between "self and self," the comic self proposes as selving.

It occurs when the I grasps that it is unequal to its contracted self, when the inherent opposition is thought and named. Selving occurs when the most fundamental "alterity" is recognized for what it is: any thinking of "alterity" must first refuse that the "same" can "merge with itself."[6] Anything other than the phenomenological affirmation of this "same," Levinas deems an "apostasy."[7]

Selving is not simply a matter of countenancing the dispossession of I from mine but rather a giving up of a certain phenomenological faith because selving, a priori, ruptures the "selfsame" beyond Levinasian recognition or "identification."[8] Instead, the comic self proposes that we see the contracted self as an object, a mine distinct from another more open one, understood in a Pauline fashion. Paul, we recall, is the master of cathecting: "I am made all things to all men, that I might by all means save some." The comic self does not contract around mine, does not, as a matter of self-reflexive self-(dis)possession, appropriate the I. Rather, the comic self stands out for its ability to alienate, as an affirmation, mine from I. Phrased differently, mine and I are unequal, involving different standards for measuring. Saliently, however, unequal in this instance does not mean "smaller" or "lesser."

Mine, for instance, might be greater than or less than I. It only matters that the mine retain its fidelity to the principle that it is unequal. The unequal functions like an unbreakable promise. Whatever else may happen, at no point will mine agglomerate itself to I. This is no mere rehearsal of dispossession. Yes, a critical part of the philosophical project involves separating mine from I, as Deleuze reminds us, but the comic self is conceptually distinct from other personae. It knows that mine and I are signifiers and decidedly not signifieds. To assign to them the status of signifieds is not only to overdetermine them by fixing their meaning in place but to repeat Levinas's incapacity to locate difference in repetition. For Levinas, identification always transverses any and every encounter between subject and object (self and other, in his philosophical register)—that is, any incidental or premediated contact between self and self. Where Levinas's thought, as we well know, tends toward merging, the comic self is the very antithesis of merging.[9]

Selving does not so much raise the phenomenological stakes as revise them. If the alterity of self in relation to other is so indisputable to

Levinas (most often going by the name of "Desire"), then the question becomes why such an alterity or, in our terms, a rupture, the dispossession of I from mine, is foreclosed so obdurately in the name of the "universality of the same?"

Delimitation or indivisibility begin and remain, for Levinas, at home. Indeed, for Levinas home models so much of the phenomenological faith that he has, and the reason is that home is the place where individuals remain undivided. For its part, the comic self is homeless. It is a paragon of philosophical division, rupturing the self from within so that I and mine cannot be homed within. I and mine are each capable of occupying a space and time, but it is a staying in time and space that is rhizomatic rather than rooted. It is mobile and operates in different spaces, moments, and ways. It is decidedly not fixed in a single locale or restricted to a particular mode.

We can sharpen our critique further. Where for Levinas difference derives always and only from the other and never from (within) the self, selving names the practice of repetition in which the self continually derives difference across unequal times. It does not require the other for difference since difference, as such, is already established beforehand. Instead, selving posits repetition as the, shall we say, background against which the event of difference can be registered. For Levinas, difference always comes after the fact—after having left the self phenomenologically untouched, pure, and more or less whole in its singular universality, a self that is free from and of alterity.

This is surprising because Levinas at one moment does incline toward dispossession in *Totality and Infinity*. He writes parenthetically: "(What is absolutely other does not only resist possession, but contests it, and accordingly can consecrate it.)"[10] We note that dispossession can only be articulated parenthetically so that it is, for good or ill, typographically contained, philosophically sequestered, even as Levinas implicates dispossession in possession. Any "resistance to possession" must, in one way or another, open the door to the possibility of dispossession. And the resistance that secures dispossession, or resistance in itself, obviates, in the first act of contestation, any likelihood of consecration. Possession, then, is overdetermined not only from without but from within by—there is no other way to phrase this—the constitutive alterity within. Resistance to possession by the other consecrates the other; consecration, in such a relation, bears on something like xenotropia, an attraction to the other that Levinas never broaches. For him, the ethical is separate, out of ethical necessity (a self-fulfilling prophecy, anti-Kurtzian in the extreme), from the erotic, leaving the affective in a relation that is at once liminal and ambivalent. The other cannot be possessed because of the role that consecration plays. Consecration is such an integral, and indeed pivotal, part of Levinas's imagined community because it enables the self to act in relation to the other. That is, the most ethical labor that the self can undertake is to recognize the other as sacred. The self, perforce, suffers by comparison, but this by no means diminishes the self's capacity to maintain and retain the other as an object of ethical possession. Levinas's is a possession sanctified by the ethicality of the other, is an ethos without eros, full to bursting with latent, unacknowledgeable eros. How does one speak here of the love that dare not speak its name except by inferring, repeatedly, to the love that dares not speak its name and in so not speaking makes audible, and visible, strangely enough, this unspoken love? Is it even love, this sonorous silence that emerges out of this Levinasian ethos without eros?

Yet, as long as possession informs the relation of self to other, the only alternative to possession will be dispossession. To Levinas, this will mean a threat to the other's sacred position. As is clear, to acknowledge and to invoke the other is to enact the consecration of the other. For its part, the comic self profanes—with violence, or with a laugh, or with both—the consecration of the other by positing dispossession as that mode which does not begin or end, for that matter, with the self.

What is good for the gander is surely good enough for the goose. Is this what the comic self does—namely, reveal the self-possessive goose as a Cyclopean phenomenologist? Again, where is the thinking of alterity? Is the delimitation as the other the double standard of alterity, the external of difference that will not extend to the I and the mine within? Levinasian alterity equips us with an outward-looking lens, training our attention on that creature who is not us, but could, of course, were the viewing mechanism reversed, be us. We see and name the creature as other, but the comic self holds out another possibility: know that it is someone else I see. A world of difference separates these two practices, a distinction to which Levinas may be blind, but of which he is not, as his parenthetical intuition suggests, completely unaware.

Selving is a difficult achievement, and the comic self struggles to demonstrate itself equal to the work of dispossession. In this way it alerts us to the true problem of the unequal. Intuitively, the comic self "knows badly," Deleuze's phrase that it is not quite up to "equal to" the demands of truth and truth as Being. As a result, the relationship of the equal to the unequal reveals itself to be a difference in kind. The comic self seeks repeatedly, albeit always fallibly, to free itself of the stories, the narratives, the fictions, that the self should be equal to, say, what capitalism would iterate as its needs and the actions required to satisfy those needs. Preeminent among them, of course, is the need that we be interested in ourself, that we are, before all else, bearers responsible for our own self-interest. The self that does not begin and end in self-interest—this is the implicitly anticapitalist message that rupture carries for the comic self.

Once again, the figure of Sancho Panza and not Don Quijote looms large in our reading of the comic self since our "heroes," as Nietzsche phrases it, sometimes take the "form of confidants and valets."[11] In any case, no man is hero to his valet. The longer he serves Don Quijote, the more Sancho Panza understands himself to be comforter and critic, squire and counselor, the latter roles developing on the principle of needs must out of the former. It is to them that we return in the following pages.

CHAPTER 9

Don Quijote's Comic Selves

When it comes to dispossession of the self, it is not Don Quijote but his squire Sancho Panza who attempts to restore dispossession to Don Quijote's knight-errant's self. Don Quijote's madcap search for adventure exasperates Sancho Panza, as does his inability to grasp or, literally, see the real. And as even those who have only a passing familiarity with Don Quijote know, the real is impatient of tilting at windmills. The repetition leads to the creation of automatons programmed by the book, as well as another possibility: depersonalization that both affirms and alienates.[1]

Sancho Panza cannot make Don Quijote see that those are not two medieval armies squaring off against each other but two flocks of sheep kicking up a whole lot of dust as they pass each other going in opposite directions. Tired of being a thing of sport for others, Sancho Panza desperately wants to break Don Quijote's habit of believing that life can be lived like a book. Perhaps with more comic grace and pathos than anywhere else, the need for dispossession in *Don Quijote* not only cries out for but demands a certain form of laughter and scorn. Don Quijote is utterly unable to disassociate I from mine, which explains why he is so ridiculous.

Don Quijote has unachievable Overman aspirations, but they are far beyond his reach precisely because he is a man of the book. He exists as anachronism; he follows the rules of the book on knight-errantry in the expectation that this will allow him to secure the outcome of the anach-ronistic books on knight-errantry that he reads. The books do little but add a name here, a battle there, all the while seeking to outdo each other in the heroism of their particular knight-errant (caballero andante) or in the beauty, chastity, and moral worth of his love. On the one hand, Don Quijote seeks to write a book that has no need of being written. Its time is simply past. The books that Don Quijote serves are, like his florid lan-guage, a thing of history, that refuses to revive itself. On the other hand, Zarathustra follows monotheism's unbreakable law. It is a/the Book: it undertakes the search for truth; the Book is for (all) Time. This gives the Book alone the capacity to lay claim to and incorporate all three of Gilles Deleuze's times.[2] Indeed, the Book is where Time begins its endlessness. However, the Book as such also expects, in its best articulation, that read-ers will engage with it hermeneutically, despite the risks of developing a "book-virus."[3]

Mired as he is in the past, Don Quijote clings to time because he is so anachronistically encrusted in the tradition of knight-errantry. Not for nothing, then, is Cervantes's narrator an amateur historical sleuth. He finds, appropriately, the "missing" history of Don Quijote, the spelling of whose name is in question, in a store that traffics in relics, knickknacks, and long-forgotten documents. Don Quijote's history is, then, from the very beginning, a history twice recovered. On this score, compare Don Quijote to Zarathustra. Friedrich Nietzsche's prophet determinedly faces the time that must be made.[4] Zarathustra locates himself in the present present, as there past and future are not contracted. No wonder that Don Quijote never quite gets that the joke is on him.

And yet, with his strategic ability to give inn owners the slip (leaving Sancho Panza to take the blows), because of the service he and the other past knights-errant provide to all of Christendom, one suspects that he is canny enough to know how to play the knight-errant game but yet too much a man of the knight-errant book to let on. In other words, he may be faking. In this he becomes the distributive analogue to the proud machismo of that old Frank Sinatra standard. While Sinatra (in a song cowritten by Sammy Davis Jr.) evinces a rugged and unapologetic indi-vidualist credo, "The record shows I took all the blows/And I did it my way," Don Quijote is savvy enough to outsource the "blows" to Sancho

Panza, all the while insisting on doing it his "way" and with nary a regret in sight.[5] Don Quijote is so much a man of the knight-errant book that he can always turn the page, if not the book, to his advantage.[6]

Cervantes's powerful anachronism makes Sancho Panza's work of rupturing of habit and reinstituting the aporia between I and mine all the more difficult. How does Sancho Panza do it? The principal way lies in showing precisely how anachronistic Don Quijote's behavior is. Despite his best efforts, Sancho Panza makes no headway. The reasons for his failure turn on Sancho Panza's inability to do temporal violence to Don Quijote by forcibly bringing the Knight of the Mournful Countenance into the present and the real.

Don Quijote's delusion, his indestructible faith in the chivalric code, his madness, and his appetite for the quest—each are bound up in the other. What they share is a repetition of expectation. Sancho Panza can see how much Don Quijote's knight-errant self is doomed to repeat. He knows that Don Quijote's repetition is modeled on contraction to the degree that Don Quijote expects the past of knight-errantry to find its future in him. Sancho Panza knows that Don Quijote will write again what must be written, this time in the personage of the Knight of the Mournful Countenance, by which Sancho Panza means that Don Quijote, with his missing teeth and molars, looks "really awful."[7] Thus is always thus. Expectations repeat. Don Quijote is the first and most indubitable optimist in all of literature. He fights a battle already lost, fights for a love that does not exist in the not-at-all mysterious Dulcinea, the hardy farm girl known to all.

If we take liberties with Einstein's definition of insanity, much like Quijote might, we could say that stupidity is doing the same thing over and over again and expecting different results. Quixotism would then name the resilience of and fidelity to repetition. To borrow a phrase from Antonio Negri's critique of the appropriation of constituent power by constituted power, what quixotic fidelity produces is "mechanical behaviors and inert repetition."[8] "Inert repetition" has the effect of anesthetizing the practice of fidelity since to repeat inertly renders the self an automaton, throwing the political effect of fidelity into question. How can one practice fidelity unthinkingly? Fidelity to repetition here comes without the expectation of a different outcome. How to be true to repetition when at almost every turn you—Sancho Panza is explicit in this regard—expect to suffer grievous bodily harm? Still, you persist. No matter how many injuries he suffers, no matter how painful the injury (an ear sliced in half, molars cast to the wind), Don Quijote always expects the next adventure to turn out well. Neither does Don Quijote do anything to protect Sancho Panza in those moments when the squire is being put upon.[9] One doubts that this is what Antonio Gramsci means when he speaks of "pessimism of the intellect, optimism of the will."[10]

Sancho Panza knows better, but that is not enough to secure the rupture of Don Quijote's dispossession. The rupture moves from inert repetition, so that to dispossess in this sense requires relinquishing old habits—say, of acting as though there were no such thing as (an) anachronism. To dispossess, for Don Quijote, requires breaking from anachronism. The rupture is from anachronism, in response to Don Quijote's determined attachment to being unequal, given how much he has lost touch with reality.

In these terms, Don Quijote iterates the comic self to the degree that one self is insufficient to the task of rupture. It requires two literary dramatis personae to articulate rupture, and even then, only one of the selves is party or privy to the process. In everyday parlance, we call this therapy.[11] More importantly, let us note our uncertainty when it comes to designating Don Quijote as I or Sancho Panza as mine. Although the temptation is always to cast Sancho Panza as the figure who is possessed—he is in Don Quijote's unremunerated employ, an economic and moral fate he is wont to remark upon, always ruefully—we know enough to refuse any such categorization. After all, only Sancho Panza understands and speaks the language of dispossession. Alas, Sancho Panza's toil never ends, even in those moments when he nearly undermines all his master's pretensions. "It seems to me, señor," Sancho Panza inveighs in a tone dripping with scorn and ridicule, "that all these misadventures that have happened to us lately have been a punishment for the offense your worship committed against the order of chivalry by not keeping the oath you made not to eat bread off a tablecloth."[12] This is outright mockery, and a subversive one at that, which can only derive from an intimate observer who has quickly educated himself in the mores of his master's books.

Clearly, Sancho Panza bears little resemblance to *The Tempest*'s

Caliban, a colonized subject made abject by language: "You taught me language; and my profit on 't/Is, I know how to curse, the red plague rid you,/For learning me your language!"[13] Caliban reframes the notion of rupture such that dispossession becomes its instrument thanks to language, even if it is one capable of creating the monster.[14] While Sancho Panza is no Caliban, justifiably angry at his dispossession (his lineage denied: "Thou didst prevent me; I would peopled else/This isle with Calibans"), they are both subjects-become-masters of language.[15] Caliban speaks the incipient language of anticolonialism, making ex post facto of Prospero's "most lying slave" a figure eagerly taken up by postcolonialist critics.[16] Sancho Panza's comic self meets its limit in Don Quijote's anachronism. If only his disappointment had led to a different language, not simply of potential dispossession but of anger, the outcome for Sancho Panza and perhaps Don Quijote too might have been different.

Maurice Merleau-Ponty understood this. Consider how his theoretical inflection of the brutality of language hauntingly recalls Caliban's own. "Language continuously reminds me," Merleau-Ponty writes, "that the 'incomparable monster' I am when silent can, through speech, be brought into the presence of another myself, who re-creates every word I say and sustains me in reality as well."[17] Caliban, we might say, is *The Tempest*'s "'incomparable monster,'" the subjugated "savage" (as Stephano calls him) who brings to the fore the capacity of language to alienate him from his own history—the consequence of having learned Prospero's language.[18]

Alienation is tricky, though. Merleau-Ponty describes a "speech" that brings the self "into the presence of another myself." This self cannot be said to possess itself, even as it "re-creates every word I say." Merleau-Ponty goes further. If the I that is not-I mimics "every word," and the time available between this not-I's repetition of the I is short, then the I and the not-I are indistinguishable. Reality lies in the interval of time that punctuates the I's speech from that of the not-I. Clearly, we are in the realm of an illogic, since such a statement would raise the prospect of a speech not so much without a speaker but that inclines toward declaring all speech to be modeled on the dispossessive technique of the comic self. In such a scenario, the I-not-I would approximate the ruptured, discontinuous relationship between I and mine. Essentially, Merleau-Ponty proposes a variant of affirmation through alienation, one that works through the force of "re-creation." The comic self alienates I from mine, attempting to access reality by increasing the interval between the two acts. In the making-again of language, there is at once the affirmation of that language as well as alienation through that language. On this note, we cannot help noticing the circularity between the I and not-I. If we are to affirm, we need alienation, since this is the only way in which the self can have access to language. The self speaks the language of dispossession in a double register that affirms and alienates not by turns but in the same act of speaking: the comic self speaks as the I that is I and is not-I. It speaks from the position of an I whose mine often goes missing. It is the affirmation of the self through the alienation of the self. In other words, the comic self fleshes out and literalizes Merleau-Ponty's "depersonalization."

With this foray into the registers of alienation and affirmation complete, we can now draw the squire Sancho Panza even closer to the hidalgo Don Quijote. Sancho Panza knows the code of knight-errantry. It is precisely because he does that he fails to echo Don Quijote but rather subverts it in a spirit of subalternity. Through his re-creation of the substance of what Don Quijote says, Sancho Panza fashions the "incomparable monster" within each through language. An incomparable intimacy follows. By puncturing the relation between I and mine, Sancho Panza makes visible and risible to Don Quijote what dispossession looks like. Not monstrous on the order of Prospero's fear of miscegenation—we recall Prospero's horror in recognizing Miranda as key to peopling Caliban's isle with numerous little Euro-Caribbeans—but monstrous in its ability enforce the I into linguistic distinction from mine, with effects that massively disconcert and disrupt. In its own way, only when there is a rupturous language that can bear affirmation through alienation can the monstrous be effected.

Here we confront the demonstration of Sancho Panza as linguistic agent provocateur thanks to his "improbable intimacy" with Don Quijote. Sancho Panza is perfectly capable of undermining Don Quijote through discursive inservility.[19] He is the squire who speaks out of turn, who regularly flouts the "laws of chivalry," and who is not averse to using Don Quijote's fanciful notions against him.[20] True too, Sancho Panza is no slouch when it comes to undermining himself. He fears so many little things, being alone in the dark the most humorous. In one misadventure, Sancho Panza relieves himself just a few feet away from Don Quijote, rather than do so at the privacy of greater remove, because of his fear of the dark. Sharp of hearing and keen of smell, even as his faculty of reason is diminished, Don Quijote chides Sancho Panza on his poor bodily hygiene. Through a kind of picaresque osmosis, Sancho Panza has absorbed the rules of knight-errantry and, in strategic moments, turns Don Quijote's infelicities against him by revealing their ridiculousness: "not to eat bread off a tablecloth" comes to mind.

Fully able to see the knight-errant wheat for the chaff, Sancho Panza has difficulty making sense of Don Quijote's continuing delusion: his refusal to acknowledge the real let alone engage with it. After all, on their wanderings it is Sancho Panza alone who can attest to the unreality of Don Quijote's claim to knight-errantry. However, for all his being rooted in the real, Sancho Panza is himself not averse to the lure of illusory promises. Not even such an accidental windfall does Prospero hold out to Caliban, terrified as the Duke is about his daughter Miranda's physical proximity to this "Abhorred slave."[21] Who would blame Sancho Panza for holding out the hope of a small dominion and the prospect of a less labor-intensive lifestyle? Surely, he deserves something in return for the hardship he is made to endure, and certainly more than just the occasional pilfered recompense.

If the real means to suffer injury and insult and to endeavor to always set the historical record straight and if the unreal names the quixotic quest for an anachronistic mode of being, then both find themselves in flux in Sancho Panza. For his part, Don Quijote incarnates the repetition of expectation; he is where, as Negri might have it, the "myths and legends of the chivalric era are recomposed in a new fantastic figure that marks an absolute novelty."[22] Pace Negri, we might say that Don Quijote is that "fantastic figure" in whom the myths and legends of the chivalric era seem to decompose the battered body, the mournful countenance, the historical cluelessness that drifts amiably into farce rather than "recompose." Don Quijote's chivalric figure acts so ludicrously, bears himself so ineptly, persists in such unreality, that all who encounter him applaud chivalry's death.

Why? In our view, Don Quijote has something distinctly comic about him. It will not be found in the ease with which others laugh at Don Quijote's ridiculous life lived as anachronism. Nor will it be found in the repeated scenes in which Cervantes shows the abyss between Don Quijote's ends and the means at his disposal to continue his knight-errantry. If the novel pushes the comic self into the spotlight, it will be found in Sancho Panza's ongoing dispossession of a life that at times belongs and does not belong to him. Moreover, Sancho Panza's deep grounding in the real anchors Don Quijote and allows for the emergence of a sometimes-incipient comic self, even if that self cannot rein him in. Yet the comic self in the novel is not up to the mission of the comic.

In Don Quijote, repetition without a difference wins out over rupture. Old habits, by which we mean habits so old and outdated they can only be learned from a book, die hard. In fact, since Don Quijote is still with us, these habits may in truth be indestructible. In Don Quijote, the comic would be equal to the comic self if Sancho Panza had been able to break Don Quijote's anachronism, from the book and from his over-determined habits of reading, had Sancho Panza, in short, been able to sunder Don Quijote's I from his (quixotic) mine. Achieving such a rupture is impossible because the comic cannot do without ridiculing those who cannot distinguish, let alone break apart, the relation of I to mine. In its turn, the comic self is that self that points to the need for rupture, regardless of whether such an attempt at rupture fails. It is, we can agree, more likely than not to fail and it would be stupid, to phrase the matter impertinently, to expect anything else.

At the same time, we might propose a new definition of stupidity, one that recognizes that the comic self functions as a kind of idiom. One of the modes of expression in which this idiom voices itself is repetition. In fact, if a logic hangs about stupidity, it lies in the indestructibility of repeating expectations. In Don Quijote, invincibility marks him as he sets off yet again on one more adventure. With that said, this purportedly new explication sounds uncannily like the old definition we first delineated. And that may be the very point of stupidity. No wonder the comic self has its work cut out and no wonder that it speaks the idiom of stupidity, since it repeats fully in the knowledge that no difference is likely. Everywhere the self turns, there it is—stupidity. To (mad)cap it

all, stupidity or Stupidity or the knight-errant of Stupidity bosses Sancho Panza around.

The thing of it is, though, if you tell your boss that he is stupid, especially when he is, by at least one definition, stupid, he will likely fire
you—or beat you for your insolence and for not observing the proto-
cols that govern knight-errantry. And the reason is simply that you do
not know what you have shown yourself to know. In the case of Sancho
Panza, his stupidity rises to the level of Nietzsche's (stupid) animal who
would "pause its reason" in order to protect its young.[23] In the light of
such stupid actions, things get worse: "The animal becomes more stupid
than usual just like those who are noble and magnanimous."[24] Stupidity
exacts a price in "nobility and magnanimity": The "noble person [is] a
fool." Nevertheless, Nietzsche's rendering of stupidity contains within
it a kernel—it is only a kernel—of potential redemption: every now and
then there can be found within stupidity a grain of virtue. Sometimes the
"noble person" is a "noble person."

Thus, it may very well be that getting fired would not have been the
worst fate for our loyal, comic squire, Sancho Panza, since he, like many
of us, surely warms to the prospect of Nietzschean solace. Intrigued and
drawn along as he is by prospect of material improvement in his life, Sancho Panza can never get his timing quite right, although the thought of
just returning to his modest home is never far from his thinking.

However, home offers no guarantee of restoring Don Quijote's reason, nor would it signal for him the end of expectation. Was it not there
that the repetition of expectation first took root when the capacity for
chivalric innovation and imagination, as in the work of thinking, of creating anew, of finding new possibilities for the old, first met their end?
Home is where reason is trampled upon and discarded. Home is where
desire, in the most banal sense, obtains, but always of course as absence—
desire as the longing for that which can never be. Cervantes adds the cruel
Nietzschean twist to this absence. Let us acknowledge once and for all
that there will be no eternal return of the same.

Don Quijote's only possible return home would be to a home of
his own knight-errant making. It would necessarily be constructed on a
vastly different scale, in every register: a castle and not a modest abode.
He would be sovereign and not some lowly master with a single servant

to attend to his and his niece's needs. A coterie of attendants would at-tend him, always poised to do his bidding. He would no longer live the life of a lonely bachelor passing his time with the local parish priest. He would entertain on the order of the court of a brave and renowned king. In other words, he would abandon home to the past and a future would open to him. When Don Quijote possesses this future, mine will extend both backward and forward. Backward to King Arthur and his Knights of the Round Table and forward to the moment when Arthur has finally found his most worthy heir. "Knight of the Sad Face" no longer names Don Quijote, since he will excel to such an extent that even Arthur will have to acknowledge the equality in their standing.[25] If nothing else, Don Quijote shows us how difficult it is to return to the past in a straight line.

Given the opening of such grandiose vistas, it is no wonder that, here again, the comic wins out. Once more, Don Quijote's unreal time always manages to hold the upper hand. Sancho Panza simply cannot ground his master in the real and, we should add, sometimes himself: the odd cache of gold crowns will mess with a squire's head, will loosen, for a brief mo-ment, his own hold on the real.

Where does this foray into Don Quijote's repetition leave us? To the degree that the comic self requires two selves, one to be stupid and the other to point out, again and again until the end of life, that the other is being stupid, the Sisyphean role belongs to the comic self: to be the long-winded critic of how stupid it is to repeat without difference. Time after time, Sancho Panza has to point out to Don Quijote the ridiculousness of his fidelity to anachronism. Again and again, he exposes anachronistic ridiculousness, the stupidity that comes because it repeats past behaviors, past attitudes, actions, and dramas without any difference. On the one side, Don Quijote stands, head tilted like the windmills he resembles, upright, gazing out over a horizon that he fills with the mise-en-scène of chivalry. No breakthrough to the real will arrive despite all of Sancho Panza's ministrations. On the other, Sancho Panza continues to remind him of a truth that Don Quijote cannot hear. In Negri's phrasing, Cer-vantes's "new fantastic figure" Don Quijote names the stupidity of "ab-solute novelty." Sancho Panza's role is to be the unrelenting critic of that absolute novelty and to call it stupid. Stupid is as stupid does.

CHAPTER 10

The Unequal

To know the self as unequal is to know that the self is not the same across past, present, and future.[1] As a Deleuzian proposition, it means to live with an understanding of equal and unequal that makes difference an infinitely multiplying difficulty—a difference to be thought again and again. Gilles Deleuze frames his proposition succinctly: "Equal being is immediately present in everything, without mediation or intermediary, even though things reside unequally in this equal being."[2] We are freed from the supposition that "all things are equal" as this "being equal" is not only present but unmediated, as long as we can nominate how and in what measure the unequal past, present, or future comes to constitute the equal. In deciding how each unequal constituent aligns itself with every other unequal thing, we are called upon first to account for how it is we disarticulate things from being. In a word, we carefully designate each unequal thing and delineate how it makes up the whole, all this while beginning from a proposition of the equal that is already on the precipice of rearrangement—that is, on the cusp of making itself unequal in its unequal equalness.

Clearly, the concept of the unequal remains among the most difficult in Deleuze's lexicon. Our critique of Don Quijote in the previous chapter offered our first iteration of it, when Sancho Panza as comic self is unequal to the comic in Don Quijote: Sancho Panza continually fails to break his knight-errant's sedimented relation to tradition and the past. In this chapter, let us initially propose the following: the unequal provides the challenge of breaking with possession, and hence repetition, and so sets up for failure those who attempt dispossession of any sort, let alone the self. To be knowingly set up, to know the outcome in advance, dooms the comic self like so many poetic personas of an Olde English poem. "The Wanderer" and "The Seafarer," insofar as inexorability marks them from the opening stanzas, spring quickly to mind.[3]

The key to residing unequally across past, present, and future lies in understanding the notion of equal being as having levels, which allow, say, in moments of grace or profound joy, for it to be present to itself in everything. Mediation, senses, and screens are torn away in these moments—if need be, rudely. Previous perforation has been destroyed, which is enacted more or less violently. Once the destruction (or *Dekonstruktion,* as Martin Heidegger would prefer) has taken place, the Being that joins everything becomes visible to being. To be clear, the directness of access is not to my being but to the Being of which my being is a part. (In classical Heideggerian terms, this is the being of Being, or, more clinically, my being's Being.) As we know, Deleuze suffers from an allergy to the dialectic. In order to stop sneezing, he asserts a grammatical structure we can best describe as the conditional-inflected-with-a-hint-of-the-declarative: "even though." This allows room for a potential question, makes early accommodation for a possible objection, and grants us the opportunity to engage second thoughts, while moving unerringly toward a statement. As Deleuze says of Michel Foucault, the "new archivist," "his endpoint is the statement, the simple inscription of what is said, the positivity of the dictum."[4] There is no other way to make this particular statement: the makeup of this equal being will consist of things that are settled, will consist of things that reside in equal Being.

Yet, the question that Deleuze does not ask here may be the most crucial. To observe equal being in everything, does this not require adopting a position vis-à-vis equal being that is either higher or lower with respect to Being? To which we are inclined to respond: the condition for residing unequally may be what is needed in order to witness equal being as immediately present by its absence. We can name this, as Antonio Negri does, as desire: "the absoluteness of an absence, an infinite void of possibilities."[5]

Not being immediately present becomes a condition for equal being to be present to its unequal constituent elements. What we have, then, is this. Rather than extolling the virtues of only equal being—a being that is present without mediation—we need to acknowledge, again and again, that mediation keeps equal being from being present to itself, since this is precisely what allows us to see both presence and impresence, a presence that contains within it or is fractured by absence. It makes visible to us the equal and unequal, the comic and the comic self.

Admittedly, such a representation verges on a half-truth. If anything or anyone can stop the equal from being present to itself, that entity will lie beyond them. In short, it achieves a transcendental perspective. Perhaps Pier Paolo Pasolini's imploring for the everyday of politics in his call of duty to undertake regular, mundane duty, all the while understanding that no day's work is ever the same, may, at its very core, contains just such a perspective.

To reside unequally across past, present, and future for Deleuze means identifying with the unequal. In our case, the comic self knows itself as unequal to the work of consistent, unabated dispossession and so runs the risk of continually confusing the equal with the unequal. How does the comic self know that what it takes as dispossession is, in fact, that? Again, the challenge of being unequal lies in breaking with repeatedly possessing. The unequal knows itself to be unequal to the task of opening to a presence, a presence that might or might not be Christlike, in which I as such enjoys no sovereignty over being. The most damning paradox follows: one can only possess the unequal and never the equal, since possessing generates the unequal. Of course, the irrefutable effect of the ever-increasing unequal is to put the equal further and beyond the reach of the I. The unequal removes itself into a time of its own, one that is unknowable to itself. Not able to explain how rupture works, the comic reinforces the sovereignty of I over being. The comic self knows better, most of the time, at least, than to attempt possession.

What does it mean to be unequal to the unequal or, for that matter, equal to the equal, or, more fancifully, to be up to what it cannot be equal to? It requires that the comic self begin from a point of failure in order to know what it is unequal to. The comic self takes stock without measuring, attaching itself to a *discursus* of "not being up to." It accepts that under no circumstances does the comic self want to be unequal to itself. After all, how can a self be up to being unequal to what it cannot be equal to? The thought that presents itself, urgently, is this: the comic self is not up to the task of dispossessing.

In the essay "Personal Identity," Derek Parfit offers insights that resonate with Deleuze's work on the temporality of difference or vice versa. Here Parfit uses Marcel Proust's *Remembrance of Things Past,* a novel that incidentally looms large in *Difference and Repetition* as well, in a register that echoes our earlier thinking of the comic self.[6] Parfit argues:

> Although Proust distinguished between successive selves, he still thought of one person as being these different selves. This would not do on the way of thinking I propose. If I say, "It will not be me, but one of my future selves," I do not imply that I will be that future self. He is one of my later selves, and I am one of his earlier selves. There is no underlying person who we both are.[7]

The contracted self that is distinguished from its earlier self explains precisely why Deleuze requires the impersonal: it is only through the impersonal that the later self can be kept apart and can disavow, in advance, an earlier self.

There is "no underlying person" that I cannot claim to what I would later want to name "mine," where what I understand to be later, however much later, is neither here nor there. Dispossession denies the I any sovereignty over what I would like to claim as mine, since sovereignty, as Foucault and Giorgio Agamben each in his own way shows us, designates ownership of, eminent domain over, and possession of. It is only a single, unruptured, entirely whole I who is disposed not only to make such a claim but to ground that claim in the selfhood of an underlying person. Such an underlying person is the figure of the self that is of and for all time. By focusing on the perception of an underlying person, Parfit seeks to undo the relation of self to the unequal, much as Deleuze invites the cataloging of the things that "reside unequally in this equal being." The subject of the unequal comes into its differentiated own because of the signal importance Parfit assigns to temporality.

For his part, Deleuze confronts philosophy with a self inescapably tied to the formidable logic of the unequal. Nothing, we can be sure, is so unequal and, because of this, so resonant with the prospect of the multiple as that which is "unequal to the unequal in itself." Such a self has no choice but to account for its unequalness, which demands that it explain how and why it is unequal to the unequal. Rendering the unequal in this way pushes it beyond what is merely Heidegger's "bridge across."[8] It is our first encounter with a self so divided that it (alone) is capable of not only undoing itself but undoing itself and, in the very same gesture, drawing into itself the most sought-after secrets of history. As a further result, this self attracts a cadre of revolutionaries gathered by, no doubt, the spirit of their plebian-ness. The gravitational force of the sublime image calls to them with the promise that begins from the premise of a disordered time in which the unequal in itself prevails. A chronotopia indelibly marks such a time, as does its counterpart, chronophobia.

The already-Overman might be that figure who reorders time and recognizes the fractured I as fundamental, presenting us with the possibility to at once submerge the self in the eternal recurrence of the same, while offering the prospect of fracturing that pattern. In such a register, time is always at risk, since it can be lost or fully envelop the self, say, through love. This explains how the comic self might present itself, however disingenuously, as a common descendant of the already-Overman, emerging out of the fracture that we will name chronotopia/chronophobia. This would be the fear of an irredeemable loss of time, since there is never enough of it (time), and of love for time since it is freed from the threat of possession. Such an account of time iterates the comic self as a site of the chronotopic-chronophobic.[9]

The figure who declares itself in favor of no-names, who divides time, sometimes purely on a whim, who unites time as/out of the fracture, who forswears family, who fancies itself as a Spartacus-to-whom-the-plebians'-secret-is-entrusted, and who, most of all, is intrigued and not in the least intimidated by Deleuze's formula ($= \neq$)—this is the comic self. Here difference, whether acknowledged or not, seeks its own dissolution, in such a way that the G. W. F. Hegel of *Aesthetics* would surely agree with, in order to put an end entirely to all and every difference. Through the comic self, it becomes possible to dissolve in a Hegelian fashion the distinction between comedy and tragedy that so preoccupies his *Aesthetics*. The dissolution to which the comic self so insistently inclines is the resolution that can be, incipiently, traced to Hegel's *Aesthetics*.

Chronophobia? Chronotopia?

Such a reading of the comic self who divides time as a way of dispossessing it has remarkable political effects. "Consider carefully," Deleuze reminds us, "Marx's theory of historical repetition," which appears in *The Eighteenth Brumaire of Louis Bonaparte*.[10] Deleuze employs the *Eighteenth Brumaire* to develop a theory of comic repetition as lack or inadequacy, a theory in which Deleuze both acknowledges the importance of Marx's thinking while critiquing Marx for not fully addressing the "temporal order."[11] Deleuze interprets Marx:

> Repetition is comic when it falls short—that is, when instead of leading to metamorphosis and the production of something new, it forms a kind of involution, the opposite of authentic creation. Comic travesty replaces tragic metamorphosis. However, it appears for Marx this comic or grotesque repetition necessarily comes after the tragic, evolutive and creative repetition ("all great events and historical personages occur, as it were, twice ... the first time as tragedy, the second as farce"). This temporal order does not, however, seem to be absolutely justified. Comic repetition works by means of some defect, in the mode of the past properly so called. The hero necessarily confronts this repetition so long as "the act is too big for him."[12]

The "hero" is at the mercy of time. After all, the idiomatic, "the act is too big for him," has a corollary in which time vitiates personal shortcoming: the "moment was too big for him." Time steals, overwhelms, finds the hero unequal to the demands of the moment. In chronologizing the act, the hapless hero disappears from view, diminished by a dimension over which he has no power—a dimension that renders him helpless in the face of the act. Time now towers over him, reducing him to historical afterthought.[13] The hero is not, in our vernacular, "up to the moment."

The hero repeatedly falls short, descending to the level of the comic self. There is, as we well know, nothing new about again and again falling victim to the vagaries of time—to being shunted, back and forth, between the struggle against time, chronophobia, and the impossible reaching for the time that is not-yet. (That struggle that is, in one way or another, the very stuff of Heidegger's *Being and Time*.) Time beckons from just beyond the horizon of its own possibility, calling out to be captured, while resisting any such enclosing. A deep love for and, simultaneously, an even deeper fear of time marks the hero.

Chronophobia manifests itself most obviously in the attempts by the comic self to be free from time's bondage. Doing so, it explicitly acknowledges the benefits of dispossession and so practices a love of self based entirely on the self's fear of time. In such a moment, the point of arrival would be the iteration of the present present that happens when belief in the future militates against eternal return. Only belief in the future and a future exempt from the status and the demands of the present present can end the cycle of endless repetition in a lineage that stretches back at least to Socrates and runs purposely through Friedrich Nietzsche, Heidegger, and beyond, well into our moment.

Yet, stuck in the mode of repetition also makes clear how the "comic repetition" produces a "kind of involution, the opposite of authentic creation."[14] Entangled in a web of its own making or, possibly, the making the others, the force of involution is so great that the comic self understands that its defect arises out of the past where it is held. Furthermore, the "past properly so called" constitutes the (real) travesty against the comic self. Under no circumstances will we say that the temporal disorder can be absolutely justified. In light of this, we are left to conclude that time is the mortal enemy of the comic self, a fate made all the more cruel by comic repetition.

If there are names equal to the hero's condition, they are chronotopia and chronophobia.[15] The act will always be too big, as the hero is trapped between fear of time and his desire for a time that is not-yet, and to which he will not belong. The best that the hero can do is announce his desire to belong to a future that will never be or a future in which he will never be, most especially because it is a time beyond him. Consequently, the hero wants nothing so much as to be released from the time that is the present that is not the present present. The hero bets everything on time. Only in the unattainable chronotropic future will he be equal to the act.

Only the time denied him can raise him from his current status to a future equality. Then in a (unattainable) nonchronophobic and nonchronotopic time can the hero be released from the purgatory of comic repetition. This is of course a condition that is conditioned by tragedy, a tragedy that must put us in mind of, yes, comic repetition and comic travesty. Once more, it is Deleuze who charts for us the path from Hegel, revealing us to the comic self in the full complexity of its relationship to time.

CHAPTER 11

Tragic Repetition

Karl Marx's *The Eighteenth Brumaire of Louis Bonaparte* tells us that tragedy repeats itself and that the tragedy of tragedy's repetition is historic even if it does not rise to the level of "history" as such.[1] Marx condemns tragic repetition not only to "farce" but to the very repetition that Marx, one suspects, wants so badly to avoid. Tragic repetition is tragic because it fails to see, when Marx so clearly expects that it should, the series of events as repeatable, as being doomed to repeat itself once more. "Alas, poor Yorick," we are tempted to remark ruefully, in much the same spirit that Gilles Deleuze finds "Polonius' murder by mistake comic."[2] In fact, we could justifiably propose Yorick and Polonius as, after a fashion, two Shakespearean figures who, at once, anticipate (Polonius) and succeed (Yorick) each other and who (both), in Immanuel Kant's sense, form the "basis for the apodeictic principles about relations of time."[3] As Kant might say, they are "linked with a consciousness of their necessity," of the dramatic ways in which they figure axiomatically: each reminds us of the extent to which the "time is out of joint."[4]

Not to put too fine a point on it, but Polonius's fatal "metamorphosis" into Yorick becomes a claim only if we hold the etymological metamorphosis as a "profound change in form in the life of an organism" and "transformation" in tension with its Deleuzian iteration. As we noted in the previous chapter, when defining the "past or the before," Deleuze distinguishes between three forms of time, the first two of which will again occupy us directly here. The first "before," we recall, names that moment in which the "imagined act is supposed 'too big for me'"; the second time marks the "becoming-equal to the act," when the "hero becomes 'capable' of the act."[5]

The act is always—and the temptation is to say so with mirthful glee—"too big" for Polonius. At no point in *Hamlet* does Shakespeare come close to suggesting that Polonius is capable of the act, let alone of "becoming-equal" to it; even memorability, such as is uttered in the line "Alas, poor Yorick," lies beyond his grasp. Perhaps we might even say, "Alas, poor Polonius," though it lacks the same poetic and tragic ring. Instead, Polonius leaves us with a series of bromides: "Neither a borrow nor a lender be," "Give every man thy ear but not they voice," and, most famously, "This above all: to thine own self be true."[6] Let us call this what it is: advice devoid of substance; evasion of judgment, a call for economy for its own sake; and, worst of all, a "self" advised to be "true," all while obviating any sense of what set of values might constitute said self.

In no small measure, the act is too big for Polonius because of his aversion to thinking the political with care, which is to say, not to think the political. We recall on this score that, for Polonius, any notion of politics as the act that transcends the self means to embark on a path that can lead to self-destruction (in France, where Laertes is headed, or anywhere else, for that matter). Lord Acton's "Power corrupts; absolute power corrupts absolutely," modest as it is in conceptual scope, lies in a province entirely unknowable to Polonius. At every Deleuzian level of time, Polonius is found wanting.

It is no surprise, then, that Shakespeare, with his eye always trained on the opportunity for a comic turn, even or especially in tragic drama, has such a fine time with Polonius in *Hamlet*: the deadly joke is on him, one to which Polonius is almost literally blind. This may explain why Shakespeare is not long in killing him off at the earliest opportunity. He could not bear to tarry longer than necessary with such a figure, ripe as Polonius was for a royal send-up.

From Polonius to Marx

For all its poetry, Polonius's advice to Laertes depends entirely on self-interest, since it seeks to insulate the self (Laertes) from any real engagement with the other: "Neither a borrower nor a lender be/For loan oft loses both itself and friend,/And borrowing dulls the edge of husbandry."[7] We can add to Polonius's sins his proto-Calvinism. In this regard, Polonius anticipates no less an anthropological personage than Max Weber, who holds with Polonius the importance of ensuring that all rewards are secured by labor and industry. This the path that leads to eternity for the Elect. True to the Calvinist ethic of self-denial, Polonius warns against wanton pleasure, "But do not dull thy palm with entertainment."[8] Surely, the temptation is to follow Polonius, that member of the royal house of Denmark who is renowned as being no stranger to hard work.

In such a moment, Marx might very well concur that "something is rotten in the state of Denmark."[9] He would, however, point the finger of rottenness in a locale removed from the psychodrama that is palace intrigue, murder, usurpation, delayed sexual gratification, and the like. (Or, in the case of Kafka's Gregor Samsa, it is only when rottenness—that is, decaying food—is achieved that food can be consumed. As such, Hamlet's Denmark would present itself as a stately feast to Gregor. "Something is rotten," so invite me in, the "monstrous vermin" that is Gregor would surely plead.)[10] Yes, Polonius and Yorick, each in their own way, figure foreboding, albeit the latter more creatively than the former. However, it remains an open question as to whether it is better to experience a creative death or to encounter it as an anonymous artifact, a mere skull upon which political projection, dramatic speculation, and comedic excess can be heaped.

On balance, we would favor a silent/silenced skull over a priggish, sanctimonious blowhard masquerading as a sage parent dispensing ethical know-how to his intellectually dull offspring. It is better to be an exhumed skull held up by proletarian gravediggers than a pontificating incipient Weberian given to intoning, "Costly thy habit as thy purse can buy."[11] Yet we also recall Weber's greatest reverence for work, and by this metric he would in all probability condemn Polonius to, well, go in search of remunerative, if not worthy, labor. "Get thee to a job, Polonius,"

we would have Weber enjoin. In lieu of the unlikely prospect of an em-
ployed Polonius, nothing is left to do except settle for cheap comedy-in-
tragedy and let Shakespeare's dead bury the dead.

Wherever one turns in *Hamlet,* one finds ruin. Faced with the ubiq-
uity of death, one longs, as Deleuze does, "for the third moment beyond
the comic and the tragic: the production of something new entails a dramatic repetition which excludes even the hero."[12] Hamlet is, appropriately, considering both Marx's and Deleuze's regard for the play, exactly
the drama in need of that "third moment." Deleuze defines these moments as "the before, the caesura, and the after."[13] After all, with the seemingly endless "repetition" of death, any movement toward a "beyond"
the "comic and the tragic" in the direction of "something new" is already
tragically possible; Polonius's death might be said, for instance, to inter-
sperse the comic-within-the-tragic. It is on these grounds that Deleuze
can understand "Polonius' murder by mistake [as] comic."[14] Sadly, under
these conditions "comic travesty replaces tragic metamorphosis."[15] Polonius takes center stage, condemning Gregor to his almost bare room,
clinging desperately to a piece of art to which he has, in all its furriness,
become preternaturally attached. As befits a figure so patently lacking in
the capacity for self-reflection, Polonius is, unlike Gregor, entirely bereft
of any inclining toward "tragic metamorphosis," doomed to die a silly
death because he so obviously lacks the aptitude for taking into himself
anything new that might require him to think for the first time the condition of his life. There is, as it were, nothing of substance from which Polonius can transform himself. Monstrous vermin though he be, Gregor's
metamorphosis operates in a register that exceeds Polonius's capacities,
and then by some measure.

However, if metamorphosis of any stripe, and certainly of the Kaf-
kaesque variety, clearly lies beyond Polonius, then what does not escape
him will be found in his ability to suggest through a comic bearing and
comic death that metamorphosis has in fact taken place. The "comic suc-
ceeds the tragic as though the failure of metamorphosis, raised to the
absolute, presupposed an earlier metamorphosis [that] is already com-
pleted."[16] In so doing, the comic confirms its place in history as inauthen-
tic and that the new has not been produced. Deleuze puts it this way: the
comic stands, par excellence, as the "opposite of an authentic creation."[17]

Comic repetition affirms the failure of historical creation and releases the present into the "kind of involution" in which the present can historically dissemble metamorphosis-sans-metamorphosis, where the present is free to do with history as it wishes. It does so until its signal and repeated failures slide, lurch, go gently, or are rudely thrown into tragic repetition. Tragic repetition follows what emerges out of the unmetamorphosed comic era. That era foments history into tragedy and is marked by its failure to secure a "unique and tremendous event, an act which is adequate to time as a whole."[18]

Deleuze certainly understands the event as affecting the polity. The Resurrection, the French Revolution, the Haitian Revolution, the October Revolution, and so on utterly transformed human history. Sometimes it is dramatized through and metonymized as historic figures (Jesus-the-Christ, the collective figure that is the sansculotte, Toussaint Louverture, Lenin), but the event belongs to the polis rather than the individual. However, if the event is an event for an (anonymous, nondescript, and, as such, "representative") individual, then the comic era can be said to be one in which the event takes place but does not register as event for the comic hero. The failure to identify an event as worthy of possession marks the moment of the event as tragic. It maintains its status as event, but it never rises to that status for the comic hero.

It does not matter whether the event is too big for the comic hero or whether the comic hero lacks the historical-political consciousness to process the event as event. The event is and remains tragic. Much as the event is "adequate to time as a whole," the nature and the process of that "time" is that the comic hero obtains a negative singularity. The comic hero remains the only figure in that historical moment who shows himself inadequate to that time. Tragedy is then nothing other than the "unique and tremendous event" that excludes the comic hero, passing him by and condemning him to be, once more, out of time with time. To repeat: the only time that matters is the event. For this individual or that, in this event or that other event, the threat of exclusion dominates. The tragic fate of the comic hero poignantly reminds us of the uneven effect of the event. The iconic hero's "unique and tremendous event" undoes the comic hero, revealing an instance of the logic that one man's meat (the event) is another man's poison.

Comic Forensics

The comic era designates the moment when we laugh at history because a metamorphosis did not take place. We scam history, leaving it a metamorphosis short, and so with Kafka firmly in mind, we cannot but wonder: why this fate for the comic self? In Mikhail Bakhtin's terms, we need to get up close and personal without the benefit of historical remove:

> As a distanced image, a subject cannot be comical; to be made comical, it must be brought close. Everything that makes us laugh must be close at hand, all comical creativity works in a zone of maximal proximity. Laughter has the remarkable power of making an object come up close, of drawing it into a zone of crude contact where one can finger it familiarly on all sides, turn it upside down, inside out, peer at it from above and below, break open its external shell, look into its center, doubt it, take it apart, dismember it, lay it bare and expose it, examine it freely and experiment with it.[19]

Bakhtin offers the comical as the ever-present threat of giving the finger (as life surely has to Gregor and his family, depriving them of breadwinner, brother, son) and giving with "comic familiarity," because everyone is "close at hand" and so presumably in on the joke.[20] What is more, the joke threatens everyone ubiquitously and is likely to come at you from "all sides." This is not just a literal in-your-face joke but one too close for comfort and from which there is no escape. Indeed, the violence that emanates from it constitutes the comical. Take that and stick it where the sun don't shine. How is that for "familiarity on all sides?" How do you laugh at that? You might very well have no choice because the laughter is right there for you and everyone else to see and hear.

Bakhtin's "comical" is also an object to be held up for scrutiny. Does laughter as an act of proximate violence not also incline us toward retreat, in horror under the threat of being made the object of ridicule? How much crude contact does the self want to subject itself to? In autopsying Bakhtin's laughter, turning it this way and that, taking it apart, fingering it thoughtfully, wrenching away its protective outer layer, peering at it from every which way, playing further games with it (dragging just one more joke out of the resonant laughter), there arises the possibility that such a proximity reveals the source of the laughter, and with it no determining, certainly not in advance, what the name of such a source might be. Langston Hughes warned us a long time ago about what laughter, but especially garrulous, proximate, the kind shared between (racial) intimates, might be keeping at bay. This is the kind of laughter that sends you into fits of tears because it is so damn funny. "We laugh to keep from crying." Proximate, intimate laughter draws everyone in, which is the kind of familiar laughter that bears directly on the tragic. Hughes was past master on this kind of laughter, as it informed much of his oeuvre. At his most economical, a feature of Hughes's verse generally, he requires only a couple of lines, as in this poem "Young Sailor," to elucidate the tragedy that so often limns (black) laughter:

> For laughter.
> And nothing hereafter.[21]

We cannot say that history needs tragedy or dissemble that history is tragedy because of the "nothing hereafter"; that is the concurrent threat of laughter and potential tragedy. Instead, we must assert that history is tragedy, and we must guard against the "comic travesty [that] replaces tragic metamorphosis."[22] It is always better to live in times of "tragic metamorphosis" than not, since only then can we be sure of the possibility of the "unique and tremendous event" and that our time is "adequate as a whole." In other words, to present an entirely artificial choice, it is Kafka rather than Shakespeare; Gregor wins out, handily, over Polonius; in other words, tragic metamorphosis alone offers the prospect of an inhabitable present. But the comic self misses the event because it has such a bad memory. In fact, both the terms strike it as ridiculous, a point Bakhtin quickly reminds us of: "In the comic world there is nothing for memory to do. One ridicules in order to forget."[23] Need we add that such a "forgetting" by no means excludes self-forgetting, an especial violence against the self if we understand the self as the first of all events for the self. Here, of course, Kafka's Gregor comes into his own, selved, disfigured into an alien, alienating, and alienated species, unhomed in his own home, making his own home *unheimlich*. One cannot inhabit this present precisely because it varies, and among the variables it can contain will be found Deleuze's understanding of "destiny." These are "actions at a distance, systems of replay, resonance and echoes, objective chances, signs, signals and roles which transcend spatial locations and temporal succes-sions."[24] Reductively phrased, destiny names the Deleuzian present ripe for and ready to receive the mischief that seems innate to the comic era. Destiny "accords so badly with determinism but so well with freedom: freedom lies in choosing the levels."[25]

The comic era primarily inclines toward freedom and against deter-minism, always looking to bring all kinds of systems into play. It replays them so as to make them unrecognizable to themselves and to find all manner of "resonances and echoes" across the expanse of history. It con-tracts and relaxes those presents at will, manipulating them with little or great regard for how these presents synthesize themselves. The comic self dislocates "spatial locations" and unmoors "temporal successions" from their established seriality so that the very notion of orderly succession is made a time out of joint. As Fredric Jameson renders postmodernity, we might equally render the comic era an order of the postmodern, in the fatal political effects that befall a state when the order of temporal suc-cession no longer obtains.[26] When no orderly transition from one present (King Hamlet) to another (Prince Hamlet) exists—since one succession is ruptured from another (Claudius)—we find ourselves up against the most famous and dramatic punctuation in Shakespearean time. It is in *Hamlet* that determinism wins out conclusively over freedom. Neither King nor Prince can find a level at which they are free to live their lives. As such, their lives are already overdetermined by death.

Hamlet remains among those dramas in which not one but two he-roes die. Although, it could be argued, the deaths of King and Prince Hamlet are achieved by different means, there can be no disputing that their deaths derive from the same dramatic event: a fratricidal assassina-tion that amounts to a palace coup. The deaths of father and son consti-tute actions too intimate to bear. As such, Deleuze's "before" and "after" strike an uncanny resemblance.[27] This line with knots in it that consti-tutes a distinctive type of temporal sequence names the time given to us at the very beginning of *Hamlet*. "Something is rotten in the state of Denmark" speaks of a time that draws us up short at, seemingly, every turn. In effect, this is the work of Bakhtin's knot: to halt any thinking in its tracks. The knot exists as the object regicide, suicide, political disorder, and chaos that brings us, like laughter, into proximity with the difficulty and condition that must be thought. Time is not so much interrupted, though it is that too, as what holds us up. By halting any linear progression in its tracks, the knot becomes both the object that must be confronted and the technē of holding up that makes of every knot a moment of singularity. If truth be told, this is a resemblance not much altered in the caesura, Hamlet's speaking of the murder and its catastrophic psychopolitical effect in his "To be or not to be" soliloquy.

Where the tragic self is historic, inclining toward the transcendent, the universal, the nonlocalizable, the comic self tends in the direction of the localizable. It always insists on its claim upon the present. Its capacity for self-consciousness guides the comic self in all things. When someone repeats something, the comic self is alert to that difference and has the wherewithal to notice that what is different will mark a difference that is itself comic. Deleuze historicizes this "essentially 'theatrical' idea: to the extent that history is theatre, then repetition, along with the tragic and the comic within repetition, forms a condition of movement under which the 'actors' or the 'heroes' produce something effectively new in history."[28] Difference, especially one that emerges out of (historical) repetition, enjoys a comic valence. It occurs at and in the moment of recognition when the "'actors' or the 'heroes' produce something effectively new in history." Such a moment can only be brought about by Deleuze's theater of repetition, when the heretofore actors impose themselves upon our thinking and, in the process, we find ourselves no longer facing actors but heroes. These actors release us, as it were, from ourselves in and through repetition. In submitting to its effects, it becomes possible to experience release from the self that allows the comic self to achieve heroic status, one derived entirely from the way in which repetition allows the comic self access—at once mediated (that is, the dialectic) and unmediated (that is, the eventic)—to the language that comes before ownership. The distinction operative here between the dialectic and the eventic profoundly separates the comic self from simply playing the part of the dialogic interlocutor with the world, the tragic self, or whatever other figure or force stands in mediated relation to it. Recognizing that language speaks the self and not vice versa, as the self would wish it, always startles and unsettles. It alienates, too. Repetition powers the eventic apparatus because repetition can secure for us "something entirely new in history" as well as our release from the "whole apparatus of repetition as a 'terrible power.'"[29]

This terrible power meets another in Bakhtin's laughter. In that laughter we find the key to understanding distance or alienation as constitutive of recognition. Why? For the simple reason that laughter allows words to be used figuratively—that is, words unmoored but not freed entirely from etymology and the vernacularity into yet one more iterative, allusive vernacular or, in extreme moments, liberated from themselves completely. Laughter throws perspectives, points of view, and meaning itself into disarray. This is the sort of Bakhtinian ridiculousness that flows, full-throated, from turning things and words upside down. From this we are likely to see not only a certain form of newness or exclusion but also the possibility of forging new linguistic associations. In poetic terms, this is how the "lion lies down with the lamb."

As Bakhtin knows, to "experiment" with words allows the speaker to play with the "modality of language and the very relationship of language to the object and the speaker. A relocation of levels of language occurs— the making contiguous of what is normally not associated and the distancing of what normally is, a destruction of the familiar and the creation of new matrices."[30] This is the language of James Joyce's *Ulysses,* Samuel Beckett's *Molloy* and *Endgame,* Gabriel García Márquez's *One Hundred Years of Solitude,* or Salman Rushdie's *Midnight's Children.* Violence and creativity; the creativity of violence; the violence of creativity—matrices that deracinate us within a language we claimed all along, and continue to claim, as our own. We remove the scaffolding beneath our feet, and we are relocated with no ceremony, from one level of our relationship to language to another, deposited not-so-gently on the one just below, or hurled down to the very basement of language. From there, we are free to wander at ground level or clamber our way back, as high as we are willing to risk. A perilous thing, this language, an intrusive force, this new set of associations, this being launched sideways into fresh contiguities.

Out of this disruptive deracination that is simultaneously an unceremonious dislocation, language seizes power for itself, reestablishing an old authority over the speaker of language. The effect remains the same, however: the language that the self speaks relocates the speaker and recalibrates how it is the speaker now offers utterances.

Out of this free fall, a cacophonous laughter erupts. Once more, the joke is on us for even so much as daring to imagine that the comic self might possess the self or, worse, could ever possess language. With regard to the latter, a sneering laughter emanates from an especial depth. What is audible is ridicule, pure and unfiltered: taking the piss out of you, as a more earthy version of the Queen's English would have it. Sometimes an experiment explodes in your face, and you are left to do the work of explaining what just happened, in a language you no longer know and certainly do not trust. Under such dire circumstances, neither the self nor any form of language based on (self-)possession will be of much help. "Alas! Poor Yorick." Or, as we have already been made to recognize, dispossession always emerges triumphant, no matter, or sometimes because of, our determination to seize control of the language that speaks us.

Acknowledgments

Tim

My heartfelt thanks go to my coauthor, Grant Farred, who in 2018 not only rescued the project but gave it new critical life and made the comic self a figure worth writing and thinking about.

I would also like to thank the manuscript's two readers, whose thoughtfulness and skepticism about some of our claims made clearer the stakes of our argument. Doug Armato was, as always, a brilliant interlocutor; our conversations gave us needed perspective on how to frame the emergence of the comic self.

Go Knicks.

Grant

My greatest debt here is to my coauthor, Tim Campbell. His philosophical range, his patience with the writing, his aptitude for brevity and his overall sense of what the project needed at exactly the right moment is something at which I continue, in retrospect, to marvel. Tim made out of a remove from that which obstructs and interrupts thinking an imperative: there is writing to be done. All this and a remarkable sense of generosity. Thanks, Tim, for making *The Comic Self* an absolute pleasure to have cowritten. On a more tragic note, Tim and I are bonded by our fatal loyalty to the NY Knicks. In fact, we may have come to coauthor this book so as to find yet one more opportunity to commiserate at the hopelessness of our fandom. Alas.

We owe our editor Doug Armato a great deal. Doug continually impressed upon us the need to write, edit, think, and then to write, edit, and think again about this project. Many of our key insights emerge from Doug's gentle insistence that there was more to be done. He drew the best possible articulation of *The Comic Self* from us.

Once again, I was able to rely on the incisive critical abilities of His Eminence, Fr. Robert.

Por Izzy, mi guapa perra, thanks, I guess, for taking me on a walk every morning.

For Jernej Habjan: archivist extraordinaire of the contemporary comic scene, and well beyond.

For Nip: who, despite his initial protests, has come to not only enjoy Cervantes's *Don Quijote* beyond his and my wildest expectations but now proclaims it his "favorite book."

Finally, to Alex: who has committed himself to writing. And who took me to my first live comedy show in Minneapolis.

Tim Campbell, Grant Farred: Ithaca, 2019–22

Notes

Preface

1. Michel Foucault, *The Government of Self and Others: Lectures at the Collège de France,* trans. Graham Burchell (New York: Palgrave Macmillan, 2010), 5.
2. Michel Foucault, *The Birth of Biopolitics: Lectures at the Collège de France,* trans. Graham Burchell (New York: Palgrave Macmillan, 2010), 226–33.
3. Lauren Berlant and Sianne Ngai, eds., "Comedy: An Issue," Special Issue, *Critical Inquiry* 43, no. 2 (Winter 2017).
4. Jacques Derrida, *Spurs: Nietzsche's Styles/Eperons: Les Styles de Nietzsche,* trans. Barbara Harlow (Chicago: University of Chicago Press, 1981), 109.
5. Gilles Deleuze, *Difference and Repetition,* trans. Paul Patton (London: Continuum, 2001), 15.
6. Roland Barthes, *The Neutral: Lecture Course at the Collège de France (1977–1978),* trans. Rosalind E. Krauss and Denis Hollier (New York: Columbia University Press, 2005), 67.

Introduction

1. Gilles Deleuze and Félix Guattari, *What Is Philosophy?,* trans. Hugh Tomlinson and Graham Burchell (New York: Columbia University Press, 1994).
2. See, in this regard, Alenka Zupančič, *The Odd One In: On Comedy* (Cambridge, Mass.: MIT Press, 2008); "Comedy: An Issue," ed. Lauren Berlant and Sianne Ngai, Special Issue, *Critical Inquiry* 43, no. 2 (Winter 2017).
3. This is not to say that the comic self somehow escapes the dialectic. Indeed,

113

in our reading, the comic self is also well-disposed toward the dialectic, since it often has a paradoxical predilection for on occasion possession. We propose the comic self as the figure for and of dispossession, as it harbors within it as well the propensity for possession, since without that dispossession would be impossible.

4. "At its plastic height in Greece, tragedy remains one-sided by making the validity of the substance and necessity of ethical life its essential basis and by leaving undeveloped the individuality of the dramatis personae and the depths of their personal life. Comedy on its side brings to view in a converse mode of plasticity, and to perfection, the subjective personality in the free expatiation of its absurdity and its absurdity's dissolution." G. W. F. Hegel, *Aesthetics: Lectures on Fine Art,* vol. 2, trans. T. M. Knox (Oxford: Clarendon Press, 1975), 1,222.

5. "Or metaphor may arise from the wit of a subjective caprice which, to escape from the commonplace, surrenders to a piquant impulse, not satisfied until it has succeeded in finding related traits in the apparently most heterogeneous material and therefore, to our astonishment, combining things that are poles apart from one another." G. W. F. Hegel, *Aesthetics: Lectures on Fine Art,* vol. 1 (Oxford: Clarendon Press, 1975), 407.

6. See the forthcoming translation of Roberto Esposito, *Ten Thoughts of the Impolitical* (Minneapolis: University of Minnesota Press), as well as his *Categories of the Impolitical,* trans. Connal Parsley (New York: Fordham University Press, 2015).

7. Jacques Derrida, *Spurs/Éperon,* trans. Barbara Harlow (Chicago: University of Chicago Press, 1978), 41.

8. Derrida, *Spurs,* 41, 109.

9. Children and Rousseau know the score: "The first man, who after enclosing a piece of ground, took it into his head to say, this is mine, and found people simple enough to believe him, was the real founder of civil society. How many crimes, how many wars, how many murders, how many misfortunes and horrors, would that man have saved the human species, who pulling up the stakes or filling up the ditches should have cried to his fellows: Beware of listening to this impostor; you are lost, if you forget that the fruits of the earth belong equally to us all, and the earth itself to nobody!" Jean-Jacques Rousseau, *The Social Contract and the First and Second Discourses* (New Haven, Conn.: Yale University Press, 2002), 113. Our thanks to Ian Balfour for the Rousseau.

10. Joan Armatrading is a black British artist who rose to fame in the 1970s. *Me Myself I,* released in 1980, was the highlight of her career.

11. Étienne Balibar, *Citizen Subject: Foundations for Philosophical Anthropology,* trans. Steven Miller (New York: Fordham University Press, 2017), 90.

12. Balibar, *Citizen Subject,* 91.

13. Augustine, *Confessions,* trans. F. J. Sheed (Indianapolis: Hackett, 2006), 45.

14. There is a long and rich scholarship on these questions. See, for example, John Milbank, "From Sovereignty to Gift: Augustine's Critique of Interiority," *Polygraph* 19–20 (2008); Charles Taylor, *Sources of the Self: The Making of Modern Identity* (Cambridge, Mass.: Harvard University Press, 1989). Augustine's *Confessions* also has a history of being thought in relation to Rene Descartes's *cogito ergo sum,* a line of critique that is indebted to Martin Heidegger's recognition that Descartes's work marked a decisive turn in the direction of the subject—a concept that is, of course, significantly older and might well begin with Aristotle. See, for example, Alain de Libera, "When Did the Modern Subject Emerge?" *American Catholic Philosophical Quarterly* 82, no. 2 (2008).

15. Balibar, *Citizen Subject,* 88.

16. Augustine, *Confessions,* 44.

1. The Sunset of the Self

1. Jacques Lacan, "The Mirror Stage as Formative of the I Function as Revealed in Psychoanalytic Experience," in *Écrits: The First Complete Edition in English,* trans. Bruce Fink (New York: W. W. Norton, 2008), 77.

2. Our thanks to Valeria Dani, who first drew our attention to the figure of anadiplosis. See her captivating PhD thesis, "Anadiplosis/Climax: Ascensions and Downfalls in Italian Poetry" (PhD diss., Cornell University, 2019).

3. Kenneth Burke, *A Grammar of Motives and a Rhetoric of Motives* (New York: Meridian Books, 1962), xvii.

4. Kenneth Burke, *A Rhetoric of Motives* (New York: Meridian Books, 1950), 58.

5. T. S. Eliot, *Collected Poems 1909–1962* (Boston: Faber & Faber, 1963), 14.

6. Eliot, *Collected Poems,* 7.

7. We do well, however, to also acknowledge that Prufrock's neuroses may have to do with his recognition that the life and death struggle around mine acquires new inflections as, and this is certainly the case with Prufrock, the end looms ever closer into view. The struggle around mine drifts, it finds new intensities, it can become more morbid, so that Prufrock's struggle is itself a thing of immense uncertainty.

8. Burke, *Rhetoric of Motives,* 58.

9. Lacan, *Écrits,* 3

10. "Linda Brent" is a pseudonym for Harriet Jacobs.

11. Karl Marx, *Economic and Philosophic Manuscripts of 1844* (London: Lawrence & Wishart, 1981), 87.

12. Marx, *Economic and Philosophic Manuscripts of 1844,* 87.

2. Renunciation and Refusal = Rupture and Rapture

1. Pier Paolo Pasolini, "Intervista rilasciata a Clemente Ciattaglia," in *Saggi sulla politica e sulla società,* ed. Walter Siti (Milan: Mondadori, 1999). Our deep thanks to Margaret Scarborough for bringing our attention to the interview and Pasolini's rethinking of the self. The translation is Scarborough's.

2. 1 Thessalonians 17.

3. John 20:15.

4. 1 Thessalonians 14.

5. James 1:22.

6. The power of two and not one marks a number of recent critiques of political theology. See, in particular, Roberto Esposito, *Two: The Machine of Political Theology and the Place of Thought,* trans. Zakiya Hanafi (New York: Fordham University Press, 2015).

7. Jacques Derrida, *Philosophy in a Time of Terror: Dialogues with Jürgen Habermas and Jacques Derrida,* ed. Giovanna Borradori (Chicago: University of Chicago Press, 2013).

8. Here Derrida's meditation on the trace in "Ousia and Gramme: Note on a Note from *Being and Time*" is instructive because it turns us, returns us, to the ways in which the point must always be thought as a circularity. Jacques Derrida, *Margins of Philosophy,* trans. Alan Bass (Chicago: University of Chicago Press, 1982).

9. Georges Sorel, *Reflections on Violence,* trans. T. E. Hulme and J. Roth (Mineola, N.Y.: Dover, 2004), 15.

10. Following Sorel's interpretation, it is the refusal to make alliances that might be sanctioned, even by a figure such as Lenin, who did precisely this in the buildup to the 1917 Russian Revolution, or that might be deemed "strategic" and, as such, advantageous, even if only for a political moment.

11. Virginia Woolf, *A Room of One's Own* (London: Hogarth Press, 1935), 150.

12. In a recent reflection, Adriana Cavarero dedicates a chapter to Woolf's *A Room of One's Own* ("Virginia Woolf and the Shadow of the 'I'") in which she carefully analyzes the philosophical import of the "I." See Adriana Cavarero, *Inclinations: A Critique of Rectitude,* trans. Amanda Minervini and Adam Sitze (Palo Alto, Calif.: Stanford University Press, 2016).

3. Elide Tragedy

1. *Julius Caesar,* directed by Stuart Burge (U.K.: Commonwealth United, 1970). Heston's *Julius Caesar* was the first color version of the film. Clips can be

found at "Charlton Heston Mark Antony speech 'Julius Caesar' (1970)," Arik Elman, February 25, 2013, YouTube video, 9:46, https://www.youtube.com/watch?v=0bi1PvXCbr8.

2. William Shakespeare, *Julius Caesar* (New York: W. W. Norton, 2012), 3.2.1785.

3. Shakespeare, *Julius Caesar,* 3.2.1806–1807.

4. Shakespeare, 3.2.1636.

5. Mark Antony repeats honorable four times in seventeen lines, driving home his point relentlessly.

6. Kenneth Burke, "Psychology and Form," *Dial,* July 1925, 37.

7. Shakespeare, *Julius Caesar,* 3.2.1617.

8. It is, in other words, "out of order": "Thinking as such, not only the thinking about extraordinary events or phenomena or the old metaphysical questions, but every reflection that does not serve knowledge and is not guided by practical purposes—in which cases thinking is the handmaiden of knowledge, a mere instrument for ulterior purposes—is, as Heidegger once remarked, 'out of order.' There is, to be sure, the curious fact that there have always been men who chose the *bios theoretikos* as their way of life, which is no argument against the activity being out of order." Hannah Arendt, "Thinking and Moral Considerations: A Lecture," *Social Research* 38, no. 3 (1971): 424.

9. *The Cynic Philosophers: From Diogenes to Julian,* trans. Robert Dobbin (London: Penguin Books, 2012), 217.

10. In calling for comedy as the mode through which to rethink "finitude," Simon Critchley argues against the "golden Nietzschean laughter of tragic affirmation, which laughs in the face of a firing squad" in favor of a "manic laughter: solitary, hysterical, verging on sobbing." Simon Critchley, "Displacing the Tragic-Heroic Paradigm," *Constellation* 6, no. 1 (1999): 113.

4. The Comic Self Is Not Comic

1. "The first condition of the comic and the laughter it causes will be that the laughing person should have some idea about what is acceptable, moral, and correct, or a certain, unconscious instinct of what is appropriate from the point of view of morality or even of common sense. There is nothing sublime or lofty here, just an instinct for what is appropriate. This explains why cold, callous, and dull people with no moral convictions cannot laugh." Vladimir Propp, *On the Comic and Laughter,* trans. Jean-Patrick Debbèche and Paul Perron (Toronto: University of Toronto Press, 2009), 274.

2. Here we might consider Sartre's *Nausea,* where Sartre's protagonist has

an absolute revulsion not only for the physical world of matter but for his own body.

3. Jean-Paul Sartre, *The Condemned of Altona: A Play in Five Acts,* trans. Sylvia Lesson and George Lesson (New York: W. W. Norton, 1960).

4. Langston Hughes, *Laugh to Keep from Crying* (Amereon, 1983).

5. See "Science Fires Back Loudly on Trump's Cure-All," *New York Times,* April 25, 2020. This is, in only slightly abbreviated form, what Cooper mimes-ventriloquizes: "And then I see the disinfectant, where it knocks it out in a minute. And is there a way we can do something like that, by injection inside or almost a cleaning? Because you see it gets in the lungs and does a tremendous number on the lungs. So, it would be interesting to check that." Forget the quote, we would say, because we do Sarah Cooper's TikTok no justice. For this, we apologize. Sarah Cooper (@sarahcpr), "How to medical," April 23, 2020, 5:04 p.m., https://twitter.com/sarahcpr/status/1253474772702429189.

6. Gilles Deleuze, *Difference and Repetition,* trans. Paul Patton (New York: Columbia University Press, 1995).

7. Jacques Derrida, "The Double Session," in *Dissemination,* trans. Barbara Johnson (Chicago: University of Chicago Press, 1981), 194.

8. Grover Washington Jr., "Just the Two of Us," on *Winelight,* Elektra, 1980.

9. Søren Kierkegaard, *Fear and Trembling,* trans. Howard V. Hong and Edna H. Hong (Princeton, N.J.: Princeton University Press, 1983), 132.

10. Kierkegaard, *Fear and Trembling,* 132, 133.

11. Kierkegaard, 137.

12. See Troy M. Bordun, "Georges Bataille, Philosopher of Laughter" (paper presented at Modern Languages and Literatures Annual Graduate Conference, March 1–3, 2013), https://ir.lib.uwo.ca/cgi/viewcontent.cgi?article=1000&context=mllgradconference. The passage from Bataille can be found in *The Abstract System of Knowledge,* trans. Michelle Kendall and Stuart Kendall (Minneapolis: University of Minnesota Press, 2001), 164.

13. Daniella Diaz, "Trump: I'm a 'Very Stable Genius,'" CNN, January 6, 2018, https://www.cnn.com/2018/01/06/politics/donald-trump-white-house-fitness-very-stable-genius/index.html.

14. Jacques Derrida, *Dissemination,* trans. Barbara Johnson (London: Athlone, 1981), 198.

15. Stewart Lee, "We Must Honour Those Brave Souls . . . Working with Ricki Gervais," *Guardian,* May 3, 2020, https://amp.theguardian.com/commentisfree/2020/may/03/we-must-honour-those-brave-souls-working-with-ricky-gervais.

16. Lee, "We Must Honour Those Brave Souls."

17. Friedrich Nietzsche, *The Birth of Tragedy Out of the Spirit of Music,* trans. Ian Johnston, Johnstoniatexts, http://johnstoniatexts.x10host.com/nietzsche/tragedyhtml.html.

18. Dave Chappelle, "Clayton Bigsby, the World's Only Black White Supremacist - Chappelle's Show," Comedy Central, November 11, 2019, YouTube video, 9:08, https://www.youtube.com/watch?v=BLNDqxrUUwQ.

19. Chappelle, "Clayton Bigsby."

20. "The reason I speak to them in parables is that 'seeing they do not perceive, and hearing they do not listen, nor do they understand.'" Matthew 13:13.

21. Constantin Noica, *Becoming Within Being,* trans. Alistair Ian Blyth (Milwaukee, Wisc.: Marquette University Press, 2009), 5. Explicating the primacy of the circle, Noica writes, "Becoming within Being, with the circle it brings about, thus implies human reality, which in its turn presupposes the act of culture, while the latter presupposes philosophical consciousness, sophia. This means that human reality, culture and sophia metaphysically sustain the world: it is not merely a question of knowledge of Being, but rather humans, culture, sophia remove the world from the simple state of becoming, they perfect it by elevating it to the level of Being."

22. R.E.M., "It's the End of the World as We Know It (and I Feel Fine)," on *Singles Collected,* I.R.S., 1994.

23. Jacques Lacan, *Transference: The Seminar of Jacques Lacan, Book VIII,* trans. Bruce Fink (Cambridge: Polity Press, 2015), 3.

24. "The purpose of art is to impart the sensation of things as they are perceived and not as they are known. The technique of art is to make objects 'unfamiliar,' to make forms difficult, to increase the difficulty and length of perception because the process of perception is an aesthetic end in itself and must be prolonged." Viktor Shklovsky, "Art as Technique," in *Russian Formalist Criticism: Four Essays,* trans. Lee T. Lemon and Marion J. Reis (Lincoln: University of Nebraska Press, 1965), 12.

25. Bruce Springsteen, "Streets of Philadelphia," track 14 on *Greatest Hits,* Columbia Records, 1994, Genius, https://genius.com/Bruce-springsteen-streets-of-philadelphia-lyrics.

26. Friedrich Nietzsche, *The Birth of Tragedy,* trans. Ronald Spiers (Cambridge: Cambridge University Press, 1999), 33.

27. Nietzsche, *Birth of Tragedy,* 33.

28. Noica, *Becoming Within Being,* 22.

29. It is also possible to translate hidalgo as "sangre azul," "blue blood"—that is, as a member of the aristocracy; Don Quijote would number among the lesser aristocracy.

30. Miguel de Cervantes, *Don Quijote,* trans. Burton Raffel (New York: W. W. Norton, 1999), 109. Jorge Luis Borges for his part will argue that hidalgo in the title ought to be translated as "country gentleman." See Jorge Luis Borges, "A Recovered Lecture on Cervantes," *Inti: Revista de literature hispánica* 45 (1997): 127–33, https://digitalcommons.providence.edu/cgi/viewcontent.cgi?article=1963&context=inti. Our thanks to Ian Balfour for the reminder.

31. John Limon, *Stand-Up Comedy in Theory, or Abjection in America* (Durham, N.C.: Duke University Press, 2000), 23.

32. William Shakespeare, *The Tragedy of Hamlet Prince of Denmark,* ed. Sylvan Barnet (New York: Penguin, 1998), 3.1.1749.

33. Limon, *Stand-Up Comedy in Theory,* 23.

5. "I Think"

1. Gilles Deleuze, *Difference and Repetition,* trans. Paul Patton (New York: Columbia University Press, 1995), 86.

2. Étienne Balibar, *Citizen Subject: Foundations for Philosophical Anthropology,* trans. Steven Miller (New York: Fordham University Press, 2017), 91.

3. Balibar, *Citizen Subject,* 91.

4. On this note, see David Hume's "pain and pleasure, grief and joy." David Hume, *A Treatise on Human Nature* (New York: Oxford University Press, 2009), 164.

6. David Hume

1. David Hume, *A Treatise of Human Nature,* Project Gutenberg, https://www.gutenberg.org/files/4705/4705-h/4705-h.htm, sect. VI. of Personal Identity. Henri Bergson makes a point that resonates with both Hume and Deleuze, if in distinct philosophical registers. Arguing in favor of inconstancy and critiquing repetition, Bergson writes: "A little reflection will show that our mental state is ever changing, and that if our gestures faithfully followed these inner movements, if they were as fully alive as we, they would never repeat themselves, and so would keep imitation at bay." Henri Bergson, *Laughter: An Essay on the Meaning of the Comic,* trans. Cloudesley Brereton (New York: Andesite, 2017), 12. "Imitation" is only possible if there is no difference in repetition. It is precisely this aptitude for enacting difference (in repetition) that distinguishes the comic self.

2. It is one of the unexpected ironies of our research into the comic self to have arrived at the notion of sovereign impressions and with it the resonances to

be heard with the Stoic Epictetus. Consider, for example, this passage: "But first of all, don't allow yourself to be dazed by the rapidity of the impact, but say, 'Wait a while for me, my impression, let me see what you are, and what you're an impression of; let me test you out. And then don't allow it to lead you on by making you picture all that may follow, or else it will take possession of you and conduct you wherever it wants." Epictetus, *Discourses, Fragments, Handbook,* trans. Robin Hard (Cambridge: Oxford University Press, 2014), bk. 2, para. 19.

3. Hume, *Treatise of Human Nature,* sect. I. of Liberty and Necessity.

4. Hume, sect. VI. of Personal Identity.

5. Michel Foucault, *History of Madness,* trans. Jean Khalfa (New York: Routledge, 2006), 136.

6. Miguel Cervantes, *Don Quijote,* trans. Burton Raffel (New York: W. W. Norton, 1999), 235–37.

7. Cervantes, *Don Quijote,* 261. For Antonio Gramsci, the figure of the intellectual is, of course, of paramount importance. In "The Formation of Intellectuals," but elsewhere too, who counts as an intellectual and what the nature of that labor is always the question of record. Gramsci works assiduously to overturn the hierarchy that establishes the primacy of mental over physical labor. As he so famously remarks, "All men are intellectuals, one could therefore say; but all men do not have the function of intellectuals in society." Antonio Gramsci, "The Modern Prince: Essays on the Science of Politics in the Modern Age," in *The Modern Prince and Other Writings,* trans. Louis Marks (New York: International Publishers, 1987), 121. Every form of labor, Gramsci insists, requires mental capacity and activity, in addition to the physical energy exerted.

8. Cervantes, *Don Quijote,* 260.

9. Bergson, *Laughter,* 12.

10. Bergson, 12. Compare with Mel Brooks's definition of tragedy and comedy: "Tragedy is when I cut my finger. Comedy is when you fall into an open sewer and die." See as well Hans Blumenberg's classic reading of Plato, philosophy, and laughter, *The Laughter of the Thracian Woman: A Protohistory of Theory,* trans. Spencer Hawkins (London: Bloomsbury, 2015).

11. "All character is comic, provided we mean by character the ready-made element in our personality, that mechanical element which resembles a piece of clockwork wound up once for all and capable of working automatically." Bergson, *Laughter,* 73. That such clockwork is easily transformed into "the subterranean, the interminably heroic production" of Pierre Menard's Quijote needs no further mention. Jorge Luis Borges, "Pierre Menard, Author of the Quixote," in *Labyrinths: Selected Stories and Other Writings* (New York: New Directions, 1964), 51.

12. Bergson, *Laughter,* 19.

13. In his essay on *The Prince,* Gramsci argues that "spontaneity," rather than being an unmediated, immediate outburst of energy (words, actions), is instead the consequence "mechanicalism"; the spontaneous is the effect of the mechanistic. Gramsci, "Modern Prince," 137.

14. Bergson, *Laughter,* 14.

15. The Dorotea–Cardenio licentiate mise-en-scène reveals that this frame applies not only to Don Quijote, and, by extension, Sancho Panza, but most of all to Dorotea, who acknowledges that "she had read many tales of chivalry and knew precisely how damsels were supposed to beg boons of knights errant." Cervantes, *Don Quijote,* 190. The comic vice, which will be used to con and coax Don Quijote back to his senses, demands no creativity or flexibility and is required from Dorotea, who steps, while missing only a rhetorical beat or two, into the role of, in Sancho Panza's description, the "'exalted Princess Micomicona, queen of the great kingdom of Micomicón, in Ethiopia'" (192). "Micomicón, in Ethiopia" is a fantastical place, to be sure, and as such a "vice capable of making us comic"; the "comic element" is borne out by the suppressed laughter of the conspirators.

16. Bergson, *Laughter,* 21.

17. Cervantes, *Don Quijote,* 194.

18. A tragic self, in other words, most unworthy of "Constantin Constantius's" (Kierkegaard's) young lover, that "young man [who] was in the wide sense the sorrowful knight of recollection's only happy love." Søren Kierkegaard, *Fear and Trembling,* trans. Howard V. Hong and Edna H. Hong (Princeton, N.J.: Princeton University Press, 1983), 146. Kierkegaard, as we well know, creates "Constantius" as his alter ego narrator in order to animate the difference between repetition and recollection. Even allowing for that, we could not argue that this "young man" has the signal advantage of at least, fictional though the terms may be, having repeated contact with his love object. In Kierkegaard's terms, Don Quijote is incapable of repetition, only recollection. For Kierkegaard, repletion "takes courage" and it is "what makes us profound human beings." However, in this regard it is difficult to gainsay the ways in which, following Kierkegaard, recollection or recollecting, as such, seems to be the paradigm in which Don Quijote fits, especially as it pertains, in a recalibrated fashion, to the way in which recollecting is offered as "eternity's flowing back into the present" (137). Don Quijote's code of knight-errantry is not of a piece with "eternity"; as such, its history is far too limited for that, but the chivalric code and Don Quijote's fidelity to it does mark a certain order of a history that flood's Don Quijote's "present."

19. The temptation to pun here is great. Don Quijote's "madness" has about

it the air of construction, so we might describe his state of being in the world as his made-ness: the world that is made by the "madness" of (the books on) knight-errantry.

20. Cervantes, *Don Quijote,* 191.

21. Sancho Panza will later be appointed governor, by the Duke, of the real-fictive island of Barataria, which translates as the "island of come cheaply." The territory is real insofar as it can be geopolitically demarcated; it is fictive in that it is not an island and has no political identity other than that assigned to it by the Duke. However, the Duke, his wife, his entourage, and Don Quijote are all surprised by the almost Solomonic wisdom that Sancho Panza exhibits during his brief tenure as governor of Barataria.

22. Jacques Derrida, *Spurs/Éperons,* trans. Barbara Harlow (Chicago: University of Chicago Press, 1978), 190.

23. Cervantes, *Don Quijote,* 192.

24. Maurice Merleau-Ponty, *The Prose of the World,* trans. John O'Neill (Evanston, Ill.: Northwestern University Press, 1973), 19.

25. Bergson, *Laughter,* 19.

26. Hume, *Treatise of Human Nature,* sect. VI. of Personal Identity.

27. Hume, sect. VI. of Personal Identity.

28. Hume, sect. VI. of Personal Identity.

29. Plato, *Symposium, Plato: Complete Works* (Indianapolis: Hackett, 1997), 469.

7. Temporality contra Cogito Ergo Sum

1. The figure, the rogue, who stands outside the law, a sort of Jim rather than Huck Finn on the order of a Zarathustra who longs for his own passing, who no longer wishes to be held captive by/in time.

2. Gilles Deleuze, *Difference and Repetition,* trans. Paul Patton (New York: Columbia University Press, 1994), 90.

3. Friedrich Nietzsche, *Untimely Meditations,* trans. R. J. Hollingdale (Cambridge: Cambridge University Press, 2007), 60.

4. The "outcast" is no longer a voyou. The voyou is always capable of attaching to an other/another, even as it can remain alienated from all, "without name, without family, without qualities," as a rebel or a revolutionary on the order of a Spartacus, the "'plebian' guardian of a secret" (which can be nothing other than the impending revolution), or as a low-rent demigod whose "scattered members gravitate around the sublime image."

5. Martin Heidegger, *What Is Called Thinking?*, trans. Fred D. Wieck and J. Glenn Gray (New York: Harper and Row, 1968), 86.

6. Deleuze, *Difference and Repetition*, 135.

7. Jacques Lacan, *Écrits: The First Complete Edition in English*, trans. Bruce Fink (New York: W. W. Norton, 2008), 42.

8. Aristophanes, *Clouds*, trans. Jeffrey Henderson (Indianapolis: Hackett, 1992), 23.

9. Aristophanes, *Clouds*, 95.

10. Aristophanes, 97.

11. To this gathering of "laughter," Aristophanes is not invited. Strepsiades's invite got lost in the mail—a perversion-affirmation of the Lacanian promise that the letter always arrives at its addressee. The letter not arriving confirms Strepsiades as unwelcome guest, perverting and thereby affirming Lacan's promise. This addressee is an unworthy recipient, and, because of this, it is proper that the letter does not find him.

12. Deleuze, *Difference and Repetition*, 298.

13. Deleuze, 298.

14. Deleuze, 298.

15. Deleuze, 299.

16. Deleuze, 299.

17. Plato, *Phaedrus*, 556.

18. Deleuze, *Difference and Repetition*, 298.

19. Deleuze, 299.

20. Rudyard Kipling, "If—," Poets.org, https://poets.org/poem/if.

21. Deleuze, *Difference and Repetition*, 298.

22. Deleuze, 298.

8. From a Terminal Walk to a Tightrope Walker

1. Martin Heidegger, *What Is Called Thinking?*, trans. Fred D. Wieck and J. Glenn Gray (New York: Harper and Row, 1968), 59.

2. In Heidegger's reading of Nietzsche, "freedom" amounts to something akin to "independence of/from time." That is, something on the order of Being, something that exists beyond the Being of beings. In this regard, see especially "Lecture IX" of Part One in *What Is Called Thinking?*.

3. Heidegger, 4

4. Heidegger, 4.

5. Emmanuel Levinas, *Totality and Infinity: An Essay on Exteriority*, trans. Alphonso Lingis (London: Kluwer Academic Publishers, 1969), 36.

6. Levinas, *Totality and Infinity*, 36.

7. Levinas, 36.

8. Levinas, 36.

9. Or conciling. That moment, in Levinas's thinking, when self and other encounter each other, the face-to-face moment when self and other confront each other, and out of this encounter there emerges one of two possibilities. There is, first, and this is Levinas's preferred outcome, amelioration: through recognition of self in other, and other in self, the possibility for violence is overcome, or it is, at the very least, significantly reduced. The second possibility is that the face-to-face encounter intensifies the possibility for violence for exactly the same reason: the self recognizes itself in the other and, as such, the self sees in the other an existential threat to itself.

10. Levinas, 38.

11. Friedrich Nietzsche, *The Gay Science: With a Prelude in Rhymes,* trans. Walter Kaufmann (New York: Vintage Books, 1974), 74.

9. Don Quijote's Comic Selves

1. Our reading of Cervantes and Panza coupled as comic self aligns with Thomas Mann's reading of the novel as he cruises to the end of the world: New York City. "Does not all this cruelty look like self-flagellation, self-revilement, castigation? Yes, it seems to me as though here the author abandons to scorn his oft-flouted belief in the idea, in the human being and his ennoblement: that this grim coming to terms with reality is actually the definition of humor." Thomas Mann, "Voyage with Don Quixote," in *Cervantes: A Collection of Critical Essays,* ed. Lowry Nelson Jr. (Englewood Cliffs, N.J.: Prentice-Hall, 1969), 57. For other readings of reality in Cervantes, we have found the following the most humorous: Laurent de Sutter, "The Quixotic Principle, or Cervantes as a Critique of Law," *Law and Literature* 26, no. 1 (Spring 2014): 117–26; William Egginton, "Cervantes, Romantic Irony, and the Making of Reality," *MLN* 117, no. 5 (December 2002): 1,040–68; John Ramon Resina, "Confidence Games and the Refashioning of Totality," *MLN* 111, no. 2 (March 1996): 218–53; György Lukács, "*Don Quixote*: Preface to a New Hungarian Edition of Cervantes Masterpiece," *Communist Review* (September 1951), available at Marxist Internet Archive, https://www.marxists.org/archive/lukacs/works/1951/don-quixote.htm; Leo Spitzer, "On the Significance of Don Quijote," *MLN* 7, no. 2 (March 1962): 113–29.

2. Gilles Deleuze, *Difference and Repetition,* trans. Paul Patton (London: Continuum, 2001), 297.

3. Spitzer, "On the Significance of Don Quijote," 118.

4. Friedrich Nietzsche, *Thus Spoke Zarathustra,* trans. Graham Parkes (New York: Oxford University Press, 2005).

5. Frank Sinatra, "My Way," Genius, https://genius.com/Frank-sinatra-my-way-lyrics.

6. What is more, it may very we be the burning of his books on knight-errantry by his niece, his housekeeper, and his priest that have burned the books into his memory and consciousness. The trauma of loss is what strengthens rather than destroys memory. The book of the knight-errant mind cannot be excised. It must, instead, be brought to life by its most ardent and devoted reader, who gives the book a mode of being, a life, and a language, an entire discursive apparatus and register, that is anachronistic and, as such, open to ridicule, without ever dimming the enthusiasm or fidelity of its most unqualified adherent. Truly, Sancho Panza would make an infinitely better knight-errant, anachronistic or not.

7. Miguel de Cervantes, *Don Quijote,* trans. Burton Raffel, ed. Diana de Armas Wilson (New York: W. W. Norton, 1999), 109.

8. Antonio Negri, *Insurgencies: Constituent Power and the Modern State,* trans. Maurizia Boscagli (Minneapolis: University of Minnesota Press, 2009), 9.

9. To wit: Sancho Panza's "blanketing" at the inn, an establishment he is forced to visit not just once, when he is maltreated for Don Quijote's transgressions, but twice; the second, when he is on his way to deliver a message to Dulcinea. Keep on keeping on.

10. Antonio Gramsci, *Passato e presente* (Turin: Einaudi, 1951), 6. See as well Antonio Gramsci, *Selections from the Prison Notebooks,* trans. Quintin Hoare and Geoffrey Nowell Smith (New York: International Publishers, 2012), 175.

11. Not surprisingly, Pier Paolo Pasolini anticipates our reading. Writing in *Petrolio,* he observes: "Well, when I found myself with these two characters, invented and therefore objectively distinct from each other, I understood that they were in reality a single character and that, if they were antagonists, their antagonism was in reality an inner struggle. Precisely because they were a single character, like Don Quixote and Sancho Panza, they strained irresistibly toward their original oneness. In order to endure being separate, they had to represent two opposite symbols of a single reality. Even so, their opposition could only be infinitely repetitive: repeated in a series of episodes all substantially the same." Pier Paolo Pasolini, *Petrolio,* trans. Ann Goldstein (New York: Pantheon, 1997), 360.

12. Cervantes, *Don Quijote,* 203.

13. William Shakespeare, *The Tempest,* in *The Complete Works of Shakespeare* (London: Collins Clear-Type, 1923), 1.2.517.

14. While we adhere to, as will be seen momentarily, Maurice Merleau-Ponty's

NOTES TO CHAPTER 9

designation of "monster," our usage of his term is inflected with and intended to signify as "monstrous" rather than the monster. That is, the monstrous marks the multiple disfigurement of the human; disfigurement in terms of physical shape (code for racial or ethnic difference, from the physiognomy to the texture of the hair and so on), in terms of language, in geopolitical orientation, in relation to power, intraspecies difference, as "measured" on a Darwinian sliding scale. The monstrous, in this instance, as the colonized or postcolonial other rather than the monster who, although it may have certain human aspects, belongs to a different (otherworldly, let us say) species entirely. Merleau-Ponty does not hold this distinction. For him, the "monster" and the monstrous, as we offer it, are of a piece. Maurice Merleau-Ponty, *The Prose of the World,* trans. John O'Neill (Evanston, Ill.: Northwestern University Press), 19.

15. Shakespeare, *Tempest,* 1.2.501.

16. Shakespeare, 1.2.496. See, among others, Paget Henry, *Caliban's Reason: Introducing Afro-Caribbean Philosophy* (London: Routledge, 2000); Jonathan Goldberg, *Tempest in the Caribbean* (Minneapolis: University of Minnesota Press, 2003).

17. Merleau-Ponty, *Prose of the World,* 19.

18. Shakespeare, *Tempest,* 2.2.504.

19. Nietzsche is more high-minded about, but no less critical of, inservility as such. "Refined servility clings to the categorical imperative and is the mortal enemy of those who wish to deprive duty of its unconditional character; that is what decency demands of them, and not only decency." Friedrich Nietzsche, *The Gay Science: With a Prelude in Rhymes,* trans. Walter Kaufmann (New York: Vintage Books, 1974), 81.

20. Caliban and Sancho Panza highlight a working difference between the tragic and comic selves. Don Quijote tragically fails to account for the cause of his actions; for his part, Sancho Panza's attitude toward knowing is comic to the degree that he cannot possibly grasp the brand of knowledge that holds Don Quijote so firmly. The truth, for Sancho Panza, constitutes an overdetermined impossibility.

21. Shakespeare, *Tempest,* 2.2.357. Desire, and the "miscegenation" that would erupt of it, strike fear in Prospero's very being. Slave progeny is not the price Prospero wants to pay for the riches of colonization.

22. Negri, *Insurgencies,* 42.3.

23. Nietzsche, *Gay Science,* 77.

24. Nietzsche, 77.

25. Cervantes, *Don Quijote,* 109.

10. The Unequal

1. For a further accounting of notion of the unequal, see Gilles Deleuze, *Difference and Repetition,* trans. Paul Patton (London: Continuum, 2001), 232–40. In his opening discussion of desire, Emmanuel Levinas offers the concept of "non-adequation": "Vision is an adequation of the idea with the thing, a comprehension that encompasses. Non-adequation does not denote a simple negation or an obscurity of the idea, but beyond the light and the night, beyond the knowledge measuring beings the inordinateness of Desire." Emmanuel Levinas, *Totality and Infinity,* trans. Alphonso Lingis (Pittsburgh: Duquesne University Press, 2005), 34.

2. Deleuze, *Difference and Repetition,* 37.

3. "The Wanderer" and "The Seafarer," in *The Exeter Book,* ed. George Philip Krapp and Elliott Van Kirk Dobbie (New York: Columbia University Press, 1936), 134–37, 143–47.

4. Gilles Deleuze, *Foucault,* trans. Seán Hand (London: Athlone Press, 1988), 15. For Deleuze, a Foucauldian statement serves a primitive purpose: it regularizes, it establishes a correlative space in which the statement reveals itself as composed of objects, concepts, and subjects. The statement derives its use and viability from these "primitive functions."

5. Antonio Negri, *Insurgencies: Constituent Power and the Modern State,* trans. Maurizia Boscagli (Minneapolis: University of Minnesota Press, 1999), 12.3.

6. Proust's novel is sometimes also rendered as *In Search of Lost Time,* a transcription that fits well with the anachronism of Don Quijote's quest even if "in search of lost time" cannot capture the temporal madness of the quixotic. Don Quijote is the comic "searching for" a "lost time" that no amount of reading can retrieve into the present.

7. Derek Parfit, "Personal Identity," *Philosophical Review* 80, no. 1 (1971): 15.

8. Martin Heidegger, *Was Heißt Denken?,* trans. Fred D. Wieck and J. Glenn Gray (New York: Harper & Row, 1968), 85.

9. This iteration of the comic self must take place in time and as time itself. This iteration takes place at once, by turns, and both at the same time, of course. This is an iteration of the comic self that repeats. It is an iteration that recognizes the singularity of every one of its iterations. This is an iteration completely rooted in fidelity to the (force field that is the) present present. This is an iteration that, with significant hesitation, raises the possibility of anadiplosis.

10. Deleuze, *Difference and Repetition,* 91.

11. Deleuze, 92.

12. Deleuze, 92.

13. Here it is worth recalling Derrida's critique of the "now," the Note, in "Note on a Note from *Being and Time*." Figured as a "point," the "now" cannot but, in the moment of record, submit to being absorbed into and, as such, overwhelmed by what has, at least since Aristotle's *Physics*, been conceived as "vulgar concept of time." That is, the time of metaphysics is precisely that time that Heidegger is the most committed to undoing, only to find himself able to do so only from within the very strictures and possibilities that are metaphysics. In order to note a time beyond metaphysics, the time of the note must begin from within metaphysics. It is through metaphysics, then, that we can best know the trace. Jacques Derrida, "Ousia and Grammē: A Note on a Note from *Being and Time*," in *The Margins of Philosophy*, trans. Alan Bass (Chicago: University of Chicago Press, 1982), 35. In metaphysics we are able to identify the "trace of the trace." Derrida, *Margins of Philosophy*, 66.

14. Deleuze, *Difference and Repetition*, 92.

15. This is, in the case of the comic self, the very definition of defect: the "repetition" of time.

11. Tragic Repetition

1. Karl Marx, "The Eighteenth Brumaire of Louis Bonaparte," in *The Karl Marx Reader*, ed. Robert C. Tucker (New York: W. W. Norton, 1978), 594–617.

2. Gilles Deleuze, *Difference and Repetition*, trans. Paul Patton (New York: Columbia University Press, 1994), 92.

3. Immanuel Kant, *Critique of Pure Reason*, trans. Werner S. Puhar (Indianapolis: Hackett, 1996), 86.

4. Kant, *Critique of Pure Reason*, 80.

5. Deleuze, *Difference and Repetition*, 8.

6. William Shakespeare, *Hamlet* (New York: Methuen, 1982), 1.3.78.

7. Shakespeare, *Hamlet*, 1.3.77.

8. Shakespeare, 1.3.64.

9. Shakespeare, 1.4.90.

10. Franz Kafka, *The Metamorphosis* (Coppell, Tex.: Dover, 2019), esp. 33–35.

11. Shakespeare, *Hamlet*, 1.3.70.

12. Deleuze, *Difference and Repetition*, 92.

13. Deleuze, 92.

14. Deleuze, 92.

15. Deleuze, 91.

16. Deleuze, 92.

17. Deleuze, 91.

18. Deleuze, 89.

19. M. M. Bakhtin, *The Dialogic Imagination: Four Essays,* trans. Caryl Emerson and Michael Holquist (Austin: University of Texas Press, 1981), 23.

20. Bakhtin, *Dialogic Imagination,* 39.

21. Langston Hughes, "Young Sailor," in *Selected Poems* (New York: Vintage Books, 1974), 73.

22. Deleuze, *Difference and Repetition,* 91.

23. Bakhtin, *Dialogic Imagination,* 23.

24. Deleuze, *Difference and Repetition,* 83.

25. Deleuze, 83.

26. Fredric Jameson, *Postmodernism, or The Cultural Logic of Late Capitalism* (Durham, N.C.: Duke University Press, 1999). In a Jamesonian spirit, we might say: "It is safest to grasp the comic self as an attempt to think the present historically in an age that never really attempted to think the comic self." Jameson, as we know, opens *Postmodernism* with, "It is safest to grasp the concept of the postmodern as an attempt to think the present historically in age that has forgotten how to think historically in the first place" (ix.)

27. Deleuze, 89. This is a resemblance that is more on the order of a Bakhtinian "metamorphosis or transformation" as a "mythological sheath for the idea of development, but one that unfolds not so much in a straight line as spasmodically, a line with knots in it, one that therefore constitutes a distinctive type of temporal sequence." Bakhtin, *Dialogic Imagination,* 113.

28. Deleuze, *Difference and Repetition,* 10.

29. Deleuze, 10.

30. Bakhtin, *Dialogic Imagination,* 237.

Index

Agamben, Giorgio
 The Coming Community, xiv
 on sovereignty, 95
African American literature, 33
anadiplosis, 11–14, 26–29, 36, 40–42,
 48
anticolonial literature, 34
Aristophanes
 Clouds, 33, 65, 69–71
 in *The Symposium,* 65, 69, 72
Armatrading, Joan
 Me Myself I, 6–7
Augustine, of Hippo, Saint, 7–8

Bakhtin, Mikhail, 105, 109
Baldwin, James, 29
Balibar, Étienne
 "'My Self,' 'My Own': Variations on
  Locke," 1, 6–7, 48–49
Barthes, Roland, xiii
Bataille, Georges, 34, 38
Beckett, Samuel
 Endgame, 109

Molloy, 109
Being, 33, 41–43, 77, 81, 93
Belushi, John, 33
Benjamin, Walter, 4
Bergson, Henri
 Laughter, 54, 56–60
Brooks, Mel, 46
Bruce, Lenny, 40, 46
Burke, Kenneth
 A Grammar of Motives, 12–14

capitalism, ix, 4, 17
Chappelle, Dave, 33, 40–41
Christ. *See* Jesus-the-Christ
Christian self, the, 19, 20
chronotopia and chronophobia,
 96–99
Colbert, Stephen, 33
comic self, the
 the body of, 33–35
 and elision, 26, 29
 genealogy of, xi–xii
 and literature, xii–xiii, 60

131

and love, 22, 80
and metamorphosis, xiii
and philosophy, xii, xiv, 3, 31
and rapture, 7–8, 23
and refusal, 21–24
and renunciation, 18–20
and repetition,2, 12–13, 35–38,
    59–60, 84–85, 93, 100–102
and rupture, 20–6, 29, 31, 63, 71,
    79, 85
thinking, 29–30, 39, 73
Cooper, Sarah, 34–39
Cosby, Bill, 33
COVID-19, 2, 34, 36
Crates of Thebes, 30
Critchley, Simon, xi

de Cervantes, Miguel. *See Don Quijote*
DeGeneres, Ellen, 33
Deleuze, Gilles
    on Chaosmos, 71–72
    and destiny, 106–7
    Difference and Repetition, xii, 35,
        71–73, 95, 97, 100–108
    and the event, 104
    and Felix Guattari, xi
    on laughter, 47, 67
    self-knowing, xii, 1, 69, 78
    and time, 67–68, 72–73, 84,
        94–95, 97, 99, 101
    on tragedy, 4, 29
    and the unequal, 77, 81, 92–96
    What is Philosophy? xi
Derrida, Jacques
    on autoimmunity, 21
    Dissemination, 35–36, 38
    Spurs, xi, 5, 40
    on woman, xii, 5, 61–62

Descartes, René, 47, 50, 67
Don Quijote, xiii, 46, 54–63, 81–93

Eliot, T.S
    "The Love Song of J. Alfred
        Prufrock," 13–14
Esposito, Roberto, xiv

Foucault, Michel
    The Birth of Biopolitics, ix–x
    on the care for the self, ix, 1
    and Deleuze, 93
    The History of Sexuality, 2
    on neoliberalism, ix
    on sovereignty, 95
Freud, Sigmund
    *Jokes and Their Relation to the
        Unconscious,* 31, 46

Gadsby, Hannah, 33, 40
García Márquez, Gabriel
    One Hundred Years of Solitude, 109
geomythology, 15, 26
Gospel of James, 20
Gospel of John, 41
Gospel of Matthew, 44
Gramsci, Antonio, 85

Hegel, Georg
    Aesthetics, 4, 96
Heidegger, Martin
    on Being, 93, 96
    Being and Time, 97–98
    What is Called Thinking? 47, 50,
        51, 68, 76–77
Hughes, Langston
    on laughter, 34, 106
    "Young Sailor," 106

Hume, David, 50, 52–54, 56, 64–65

Identity, x, 3, 5, 8–9, 11, 52, 95

Jacobs, Harriet
  Incidents in the Life of a Slave Girl,
    15–16
Jameson, Fredric, 107
Jesus-the-Christ, 18–20, 21
John, Elton
  "Don't Let the Sun Go Down on
    Me," 10, 16
Joyce, James
  Ulysses, 109

Kafka, Franz, xiii, 105
Kant, Immanuel, 47, 100
Kierkegaard, Søren, 36–39, 50
Kipling, Rudyard, 73

Lacan, Jacques, 10, 11, 15, 42
laughter, 32–35, 45–47, 54, 67,
    105–7, 109, 110
Lee, Stewart, 33, 38, 39
Letterman, David, 33
  Levinas, Emmanuel
  Totality and Infinity, 77–81
Limon, John, 46
Locke, John, 48
Luxemburg, Rosa, 6

Marx, Karl
  alienation, 23
  and Deleuze, 97
  *Economic and Philosophic Manu-
    scripts of 1844,* 17
  *The Eighteenth Brumaire of Louis
    Bonaparte,* 1, 97, 100

on *Hamlet,* 102–3
Mary Magdalene, 20
Merleau-Ponty, Maurice, 63–64,
    86–87
mime. *See* ventriloquism
Murphy, Eddie, 33

Negri, Antonio, 84, 88, 93
Nietzsche, Friedrich
  The Birth of Tragedy, 40
  and Derrida, 61
  and the eternal return, 72
  and Heidegger, 68, 75–77
  on heroes, 81
  on self-knowledge, 43
  Thus Spake Zarathustra, 72–76, 83
  on time, 67
Noica, Constantin, 41–43

Pasolini, Pier Paolo, 18, 19–20, 94
Paul, Saint, 19, 20, 78
Pantomath, 37–38, 39
Parfit, Derek
  "Personal Identity," 95
Plato
  The Phaedrus, 33, 34, 72
  The Symposium, 65, 69
Proust, Marcel
  Remembrance of Things Past, 95
Pryor, Richard, 33

R.E.M., 41
Rock, Chris, 33, 40
Rushdie, Salman
  Midnight's Children, 109

Sartre, John–Paul
  "The Condemned of Altona," 33

"The Seafarer," 93
selving, 77–78, 81
Shakespeare, William
  Hamlet, xiii, 44, 67, 72, 100–103, 107–8
  Julius Caesar, 14, 26–29
  Othello, 44
  The Tempest, 85–88
Sinatra, Frank, 83
Socrates, 33, 34, 69–70, 72, 98
Sorel, Georges, 23
Springsteen, Bruce, 42
stand-up comedy, 2, 33–43
Stewart, Jon, 33
stupidity, 89–91

thinking, 47, 49–50, 65–66, 73–74, 77
time, 48–49, 51, 53, 67–68, 73, 83–84, 95, 108
tragedy, xi, xiii, 26, 40, 44, 100, 104
tragic self, the, 3–4, 29, 31–32, 40, 44, 58–59, 64, 108
Trump, Donald, 2, 34–36, 38, 39

ventriloquism, 34–38

"The Wanderer," 93
Washington, Grover, 36
Weber, Max, 102–3
Wilde, Oscar
  The Picture of Dorian Gray, 22
Withers, Bill, 36
Woolf, Virginia
  A Room of One's Own, 23–25

Žižek, Slavoj, xi
Zupančič, Alenka
  The Odd One In, xi

Timothy Campbell is professor of Italian in the Department of Romance Studies at Cornell University. He is the author of *Improper Life: Technology and Biopolitics from Heidegger to Agamben* (Minnesota, 2011) as well as *The Techne of Giving: Cinema and the Generous Form of Life*.

Grant Farred is the author of *The Zelensky Method,* as well as *Only a Black Athlete Can Save Us Now* (Minnesota, 2022) and *An Essay for Ezra: Racial Terror in America* (Minnesota, 2021).